THE HUMAN VALUES
A Task for All

About the Editors

Professor Mulk Raj Chilana, Consultant School of Practical Philosophy, Johannesberg, South Africa and President, Servitors Association of Value Education (SAVE International). Formerly Professor of Education, National Council of Educational Research and Training, New Delhi and Deputy Education Adviser, Govt. of India. A scholar and senior Research Fellow of UNESCO for two years for studies abroad. Also British Council Fellow for one year for research and post-graduate work in England. On study tours and visiting Professor in African, American, Asian and European countries. Research Guide and Examiner of doctoral and post-graduate research candidates. Undertook research studies in value-oriented education in different countries. Holds unflinching belief that value education is panacea for social upliftment and individual flowering. Life-long education being his cherished point of action, he is focussed on assisting teachers in their consciousness raising and self actualization. Also gives high priority to international cooperation for building up global perspective in all educational acturties. As founder president of Servitors Association of Value Education, Prof Chilana is committed to heed, assist and reach to all necessitous calls.

M.L. Dewan, Soil Scientist and Soil & Water Conservationist. Honorary Advisor Trees for Life—an International N.G.O. and Founder Chairman—Himalaya Consortium for Himalayan Conservation (TFL/HIMCON), with about 40 years experience, is Retired Chief Food & Agriculture Organization (of United Nations) Regional Bureau for Asia and Pacific. He has long experience in mountain systems and has built a Centre at Village Ranichauri in District Tehri Garhwal, U.P. and is living part of the time with the Himalayan Communities. Dr. Dewan has authored "People's Participation in Himalayan Eco-System Development" and four other books in "Discover Himalayan Series" and has also written—over 100 articles and papers on Soil and Water Conservation, Watershed Management and Promotion of self-reliance in Himalayan communities. Dr. Dewan believes The Human Values Adoption is a Task for All and is Key to Nation Building.

THE HUMAN VALUES
A Task for All

PROF. M.R. CHILANA

DR. M.L. DEWAN

Published by

CONCEPT PUBLISHING COMPANY, NEW DELHI-110059

for

SERVITORS ASSOCIATION OF VALUE EDUCATION

103, C2A Block, Janak Puri, New Delhi-110058

ISBN 81-7022-660-0 (HB)

First Published 1998
Reprinted 2002

Published and Printed by

Ashok Kumar Mittal
Concept Publishing Company
A/15-16, Commercial Block, Mohan Garden,
NEW DELHI - 110059 (India)
Phones: 5554042, 5504042
Fax: (011) 5598898

PREFACE

A sustainable development with human values form the pillars of a progressive society. Sustainable development is to allow for future generations from what we preserve of our remaining resources and also how we rehabilitate the sources which have been maltreated in the past. There lies a systematic approach to the path of environmentally sustainable development that is based on the following vital ten factors:

— A result-oriented construction with villagers, farmers and all other participants prior to initiating any action.
— Stress on need-based flexible small-scale projects keeping in mind that a plan must be a blueprint and not a prison. It should be an open-book, able to incorporate new information that emerges during a project.
— Let the beneficiaries decide and the experts share their knowledge, and not impose it.
— Look for the options of solutions that can be duplicated in hundreds of thousands for the optimum impact and keeping in mind that solutions must still be tailored to suit the local needs and environ.
— Education needs to be the prime priority, particularly for the youngsters and women who incidentally are the most effective media of change, being the nodal realities of the society.
— Restraint on external inputs is very vital as it reduces dependency and increases stability. In fact, subsidies, supplements and inappropriate technology are unsustainable.
— Centre development on what people are doing rightly and never try to replace conventional local practices with new technologies and at the most they must be limited to mere supporting role to the existing ones. Imposed and external techniques usually run contrary to local systems.
— Analyse and assess impacts of proposed changes, an exercise

better be undertaken by a multi-disciplinary team with experts in tune with the same culture. These studies must cover the socio-economic, cultural and environmental aspects.

— Consider both inputs and outputs keeping in view that mere quantitative figures should not be the yardstick. For instance it has been proved in agro-productivity that focusing a single output is usually futile and not always better.

— Attach utmost importance to the participants' quality of life index (QLI). It is to be borne in mind that long-term environmental improvements are unsustainable unless catered to the poor and solve their present day problems.

Sustainable development revolves round a quadra axis of access and control, community resource management, adding value to the product and lastly, investment and economic stake-holding.

With the dilution of values and resultant depletion of resources, both moral and economic, the world is on the slide. There is a strong linkage between the human values and sustainable society, the former could be summarised as all that which makes life worthy to be lived. The human values are based on truth, the right action of the moral code, peace, love and non-violence, denoted as the corner-stones of the life's philosophy. This is the basis for the concept of desired education.

Linked to this is peace, the state of mind and body unaffected by emotional conflicts and passions. A good example is the surface of an ocean-all stormy waves but completely calm as we go deeper down below. Thus peace as an essential part of education develops mankind intellectually by controlling emotional outbursts for a balanced personality.

Sustainable development is possible only if all appreciate the need and rise to adopt right system of values. This is possible where there is a complete understanding of the need for values. We hope, trust and pray that the value will ignite the mind of the readers and urge to promote human value in all sphere of human activities

103, C2A, Janak Puri
New Delhi - 110058
Phone +0091-11-5502687

PROF. MULK RAJ CHILANA
DR. M.L. DEWAN

CONTENTS

PART III
AN ACTION PLAN

PART I

ABOUT HUMAN VALUES

1

UNIVERSAL VALUES

Source and Function

—SWAMI DAYANAND SARASWATI

What is a value? 'Value' indicates the regard for a thing, situation, or attitude which for some reason is esteemed or prized by the value-holder. The appropriate values which prepare the mind for Vedanta are certain universal ethical attitudes. In Sanskrit an ethical value can be defined as dharma. Dharma is a standard for norm of conduct derived from the way in which I wish others to view or treat me. The '*dharmic*' mandates for behaviour and attitude, though commonly found in religious scriptures, in fact, trace their source to pragmatic commonsense ethic which religious ethics confirm. In other words, my norm for what is 'proper' behaviour or a 'good' attitude is based on the way I wish others to treat or view me. What I expect or want from others becomes my standard for dharma, right behaviour; what I do not want others to do is adharma, wrong behaviour.

I want others to speak truth to me.
I do not want others to lie to me.
Truth-speaking is *dharma* for me.
Non-truth-speaking is *adharma* for me.
Scriptures confirm truth-speaking as good behaviour.
Scriptures condemn non-truth-speaking as bad behaviour.

Other behaviour norms, such as non-injury, humility, charitableness, are all based upon the same consideration of how I would like others to treat me. Thus, ethical norms are not just

Swami Dayanand Saraswati, Dayanand Ashram, Rishikesh, U.P.

arbitrary, man-made rules but stem from an inherent, common regard for one's own interest and comfort. Ethical standards are natural and universal. There may be some cultural variations in degree or emphasis but the basic standards have a certain universality.

Ethical Values: Universal in Content—Relative in Application

The universality of codes of acceptable conduct, that is, of general ethical standards, does not mean that these standards are absolute. *Dharmas* and *adharmas* are relative. There are situations where what is considered ethical becomes unethical, depending upon context. That a standard may be relative does not mean that it is purely subjective. Although relative sometimes in applicability, basic ethical standards have a universal content. There is a similarity in everyone's reaction to being hurt, cheated, lied to and bullied. Ethical standards are based on a human consensus regarding what is the acceptable conduct; this consensus is not negated by the fact that the norms may be subject to interpretation in some situations. Even such a pronounced, clear value as non-injury to myself is modified by circumstance when I willingly submit to the surgeon's knife. Such a suspension of my value for non-injury to myself or its extensions—my general value for non-injury to all beings.

Although my norms or values for behaviour and attitude, themselves, may not be subjective, my interpreation of these values is very likely to be highly subjective. My values are universal in content but relative and situational in my application of them. For example, I am likely to apply a value for truthfulness very consistently and absolutely to the words of others; to my own words my application will be much less consistent and quite relative to the situation.

In general practice I will apply values more consistently and more absolutely to others than to myself. After all, the source of my values is found in the way in which I want others to treat men which becomes my norm for 'good' behaviour. I find it easy to have others observe ethical standards, so I can be the beneficiary. It seems less easy for me to be consistent in the application of these standards to my own behaviour.

Ethical Values cannot be Dismissed

Can I safely dismiss a concern for values? No. I cannot escape from values because no one living in this world can escape relationships; based upon his concern that he may not be hurt on disturbed. From this comes an accepted canon in the criminal code; do not be an informer. The inescapability of the impact of values can be seen by considering a 'hit man.' A veteran 'hit man'—a merciless killer—does not want to be 'hit' himself. He cannot escape a value for non-injury, he can only defy it, which creates conflict even in an insensitized mind. Values cannot be dismissed, nor can they be defied with impunity. Failure to meet a value puts me in conflict with myself. When I perform an action that is a non-value for me, I create a seed of guilt, which is all that is needed to produce sleeplessness, fear and conflict. Even small lies create problems, like the lies sometimes told regarding one's age. Truth about one's age may seem a simple, unimportant thing, but small lies register inside as conflicts.

Are Values Only Mithya—Apparent?

To those who have had a little exposure to the teaching of Vedanta, it may occur that norm-breaking behaviour, that is, 'bad' behaviour may be dismissed because it is only '*mithya*', apparent, not absolutely real. To such an argument, it can be said: if you can dismiss all good acts and all good things as *mithya*, apparent, then, fine; you certainly also may dismiss bad acts and bad things as well. When I can see good and bad equally as *mithya*, values are not a problem for me. In the clear knowlege of what is real and what is apparent, my actions in the relative world cannot but be spontaneously good, because I have nothing to gain, nothing to protect. It is that clear knowledge of Self which I am seeking. To be ready to discover that knowledge, my mind must be prepared with proper values. In a mind filled with conflict, because values are dismissed or defied, nothing will happen when I listen to the teacher of Vedanta.

Values and Conflict

No one wants a mind in conflict. A mind in conflict is not a desirable mind. Once conflicts are there, problems of the mind are unavoidable: self-condemnation, regard, guilt, a sense of failure are the products of mental conflict. Conflicts come when I am unable to live up to a particular value which, consciously or unconsciously, I accept. Societal norms have a universal content, the influence of which I cannot really escape. My inherent desire to be comfortable and secure compels me to set standards for the behaviour of others, establishing a commonsense ethical code which bounces back on my head. Religion codifying society's ethical consensus into a rigid table of 'do's' and 'don'ts', make conformity on my part even more difficult. When I cannot live up to my value structure, I am in conflict and suffer guilt.

'Dropping-Out' Does not Solve Conflict

The 'drop-out' behaviour of the 'hippie generation' prevalent during the 60's in the West, largely seems to have been an attempt to escape conflicts. During the Viet Nam War period, the clash of unassimilated traditional values with situational personal values was particularly acute for young people. The response of many was an attempt to make 'no values' their basic value. Traditional values were condemned and a life-style based on 'individually', 'self-expression' and 'spontaneity' was proclaimed in their stead. This did not work. True, values led to conflict; but, as we saw before, values cannot simply be dropped. The universal content of values can be negated only if I have no concern for how the other person treats me. If I want other people to behave in a certain manner, I am stuck with a value system.

How Values Cause Conflict

When I have a value structure, which I follow in the same manner in which I expect others to follow, my values cause me no conflict. However, when I want others to behave in a certain way, but for my own reasons, I am not able or willing to behave in that way, I have a problem. When I have a value and something interferes with my expression of that value, I am in conflict with myself. What interferes with my expression of my general values? Individual situational values, linked with some highly desired personal end, can interfere with my expression of general values, when the general values have not become for me fully assimilated personal values.

The universal value for truth provides a good example of a general standard which frequently is only half assimilated:

Value: Speak truth!

I want others to speak truth to me (universal source).

Authorities tell me to speak truth (obligatory source).

Parents say speak truth.

Society says speak truth.

Religion says speak truth.

Speaking truth is a part of my value system.

assimilation:

The value of others' truthfulness is immediately clear.

I can see that false information given to me can be inconvenient or harmful to me.

My value for the truthfulness of others to me is personal and assimilated.

The value of my truthfulness is not immediately clear.

I do not see what I get out of being truthful.

My value for my being truthful is obligatory.

My truthfullness obliges my parents.

My truthfulness obliges my society.

My truthfulness obliges my religious code.

result: I have a split value: one-half personal and one-half obligatory.

The value for money illustrates the development and assimilation of a powerful, personal situational value.

Value: Cherish Money!

When I was a child of three years old, I once picked up a piece of paper. It was green, printed, very colourful. I began, as I did with every paper, to play with it. Mummy said: "No! That is money." Oh, money? I also said, "Money". But I did not know, what is this money. "Money-money-money," I kept repeating. Thereafter, wherever I saw that green paper, I knew it was 'money' which I should not touch, but I did not know what money is.

Then one day, when I was a little older, Mummy took me shopping with her to the store. I saw lots of chocolates and jelly-beans. I stretched out my hand: "Give me jelly-beans." The fellow behind the counter raised his eyebrows and looked at Mummy. I wondered why he would not give me any candy when he had so many. Then Mummy opened her purse and pulled out a piece of green paper named money. When she gave that money to the storekeeper, he smiled and handed a packet of jelly-beans to me. I did not understand what had happened, but I was happy with my jelly-beans. Next time we went to the store, she gave money and the man gave me chocolates. One day when we were shopping, I wanted a balloon. Out came the money and the balloon was mine. Oh, ho! If you give money you can get jelly-beans, chocolates, and even balloons. This is a great discovery for a small child. I had learnt that money buys things—all manner of things. Not many people understand the monetary system but everybody knows that money buys!

Later, as I grew up I came to learn how many things money buys: houses, cars, even gurus and gods. Nothing buys like money.

When I come to know how well money buys, how many things money buys, I come to have a well understood, well assimilated personal value for money.

Half Value: More Irritant than Behaviour Norm

When a universal value is split into two halves—a personal value for what I expect from others and an obligatory value for what I expect from myself—there is always a potential for conflict. A personal value is spontaneously observed for its own sake; an obligatory value is subject to compromise when it obstructs a highly desired individual end. When a general ethical half-value loses the battle to an expedient assimilated value, the half-value does not fold up and go away. It stays there as an irritant. What I call my ethical values often, in fact, are so many irritants in my heart. This is true even for the hardened criminal, the habitual offender, who seems to be totally insensitive to ethical behaviour standards. No matter what choices are made or how many times they are made, the voice of the half-value, reflecting as it does an inherent universal content, is never entirely silenced.

For example, most of us have a well assimilated personal value for money; whereas, when it comes to speaking truth our value often is general and half assimilated. When this is the case, what happens if there is a conflict between the money-value and the truth-value? What if a situation arises whereby telling a lie I can make an extra Rs. 500? Perhaps someone has offered to pay me the same amount of money for an item that I had originally paid for it. I had paid Rs. 1,000 but I easily can say that I paid Rs. 1500. For this small lie I will gain an extra Rs. 500. I know what that extra Rs. 500 can do for me, what comforts I can buy with it. On the other hand, it is not very clear to me what benefit speaking truth in this situation will be to me. Should I tell the truth or should I lie? Which value will win? Very likely the assimilated value for money will be the victor. But, all the same, something goes on murmuring inside, "Speak truth, speak truth."

I may lie but I will not be comfortable, because I will not be able to avoid what happens when I tell a lie. What happens? First, there is conflict; then there is guilt. I can ignore guilt but I cannot avoid guilt because I cannot escape my half-value for truth. Guilt is a great irritant—greater than chillies! It is a very great irritant. Once I have guilt I cannot have a fully comfortable self. Fulfilling an immediate end at the expense of a general value may bring some passing comfort but in the long run adds to the discomfort of myself by increasing my accumulation of guilts, large and small.

The Knower-Doer Split

Does anything else happen when I ignore general ethical standards? Yes, I create a "knower-doer" split in myself. For instance, when I lie I become a speaker: speaking is an action, so as a speaker I am an actor—a doer. At the same time, I know what I am saying. I am aware that what I am saying is something contradictory to truth. Therefore, I, the knower, am in one position and I, the doer, am in another position. By my lie, I create a split, a division, between the knower-I and the doer-I. Everyone has a few lies like this. What is your age? What is your income? What are your qualifacations? When I make a series of lies like this I create a split in myself, the knower being one and the doer another. I am not integrated. I have divided myself into an 'ideal' knower who values one course of action and the 'actual' doer who does something else. I have created a Dr. Jekyl-Mr. Hyde conflict within myself. Living with Jekyl and Hyde one cannot get anything out of life. It is impossible. Even in small things, the knower-doer split does harm. The knower decides to get up 30 minutes early and do early morning excercises. The doer turns off the alarm and sleeps 45 minutes longer. The knower goes on a diet. The doer has a second helping. The knower begins condemning me. I tell myself that I am useless, that I cannot do what I want to do, that I am not the person I want to be.

When I am 'split' I cannot fully enjoy anything. Even the enjoyment of food cannot be appreciated unless the mind is on eating. The relationship between thinker and doer perhaps is more recognised in the Indian cultural traditions than it is in the West. In India the mother instructs the child: "Eat—don't talk. When you are eating, eat. Talk later." in the West where talking is mixed with eating, only the first spoonful of food is appreciated. The rest of eating becomes mechanical. One eats and talks and then when it is found that no more food can be eaten, one infers that the meal has been good and that a sufficient amount has been eaten. The thinker was not present when the eating was going on, being too busy thinking what was to be said next. This kind of eating is mechanical and often uncontrolled, whereas eating when the thinker is there, can becomes a beautiful ritual.

The quality of my life always suffers whenever I become 'split'. To appreciate the beauty of life, to really be available to enjoy its comforts, I need to be 'together'. 'Together' is a good Western expression which shows an intuitive appreciation of the problem of 'split'. When my universal values are only half-values, they will always have the potential of destroying my 'togetherness', producing a 'split' in me, when they yield to some immediate situational value.

What is the Source of a Situational Value's Value?

How does an individual situational value have the power to conquer the obligatory half of a universal value, producing guilts and splits in me? We have seen that the source of ethical values is the natural desire that people treat me in a certain way—which then is extended to oblige me to treat others in the same way. What is the source of a situational value? Take one's value for money. What gives money such a value for me that I may be willing to tell a lie to obtain it? In the example given before (where by 'stretching' the truth I will obtain Rs. 500) what is gained that makes the lie worthwhile to me? Is money a valuable thing worth a lie?

I cannot eat money or admire its beauty or talk to it or use it as shelter from the rain—so money itself is not the attraction. But with money I can buy things to eat, wear, look at. Money, itself, is not valuable but the value of money seems to be in its buying power. However, if I were stranded on a desert island, the buying power of money would do me no good. Thus, it seems it must be the things themselves which money buys which make money valuable, not just the isolated buying power. Why are the things valuable? The things are valuable for me—for my pleasure, security, comfort. I value things for my comfort.

What defines 'my comfort'? Is it the 'me with comforts' that is valuable or the me who 'feels comfortable?' Is there a difference between the two? There is a difference. Sometimes my stomach may be comfortably full, nothing is pinching, the heater is working and my chair is soft—still I may not be comfortable with myself. What I really value is not mere comforts outside but to be comfortable inside. It is always my hope that the extra comforts which more money can buy for me will make me more comfortable with myself. I buy comforts only for my sake, not for the sake of the comforts. I do not buy another chair because the chairs in the room are lonely. I buy a chair because, in one way or another, I think that to have a chair is going to make me feel more comfortable, either for my body or my pride of possession or both. All comforts are for my sake alone. I choose comforts for me so that 'myself' will feel good.

So when I ignore my obligatory value, my value for truthfullness, and tell a lie instead, through which I am going to gain some money, it is because I have concluded that the money will add to my comfort; and, I do not see, in the given instance, truthfulness doing anything for my comfort. The same is true for my other situational choices. Anything I choose—anything I value is because I think there is some connection between that thing and 'myself' feeling good. The source of the value of a situational value is that I expect to feel good through exercising a choice based on it.

When is a Value not Subject to Choice?

When I clearly see that a particular choice will make me suffer, I do not make that choice. When, seeking comfort, I see that between two choices, one of them is going to bring discomfort, choice drops out. My action becomes choiceless. It becomes choiceless like the answer to the question: Do you want happiness or unhappiness? Thus, when I become thoroughly convinced that acting contrary to a general value will result in suffering for me, my compliance with that value becomes choiceless. If speaking truth is a value for me, and I am completely convinced that non-truth brings suffering, there is no choice but to speak the truth. Speaking truth becomes natural, spontaneous, my personal, assimilated value.

Any value, when it becomes my personal value, becomes choiceless for me. I do not have to think about it. The conduct mandated by a personal value becomes what I do without reflection. Matters of hygiene are good everyday examples of personal assimilated values: even though I may be quite hungry, I do not consider picking up and eating food from a garbage heap; nor, do I have a daily debate with myself over whether to brush my teeth or take a bath. Conforming to these values creates no conflict whatsoever for me.

Seeing the Value of a Value

A value, any value, universal or situational, is a value for me only when I see the value of the value as valuable to me. Me—the comfortable me—is the source of my values. I fail to follow a universal value only when I do not clearly see its value to me. I make expedient situational choices only when I think such choices will make me feel good.

Returning to the Rs. 500 gained by a small lie, what is the actual worth of that lie to me? That small lie, joining its fellows in my mind, would cost me my life (my comfortable self). The extra comforts that I could buy with the Rs. 500 acquired through the lie would not be able to deliver their comfort because of guilt and split. Guilt comes because I have a half-value for truth which, when I ignore it, is sufficient to create a problem for me. Split comes because I know I am obliged to tell the truth, and I am doing something else. Once I have guilt—once I am split, I cannot have a comfortable self.

For comforts to be enjoyed, I must be there to enjoy them; when I am split with guilt, I am rarely anywhere but with my anxieties, regrets and guilts. Not recognising the problem for what it is, I seek more comforts to ease my uncomfortable mind; or, I try to find some method for turning off this conflicting mind and its brood of guilts. Thus, it is that when I tell a lie, I add to the discomfort of myself when what I am trying to gain by the lie is to add to the comfort of myself. This is true for any choice I make which conflicts with a universal ethical standard. The sought-for comfort, prompting the conflicting choice, cannot be enjoyed due to guilt and split arising from the conflict. When I clearly see this fact, I will see the value to me of applying universal ethical standards to myself. My half-value for universal values will become full value.

Life Expression Comes from Value Structure

The expression of my life is just the expression of my well assimilated value structure. What I do is but an expression of what is valuable to me. Other people's values I follow from time to time when it is convenient; but, if these values of others have not been assimilated by me, they are simply obligatory values and do not reflect my value structure. They are more a source of conflict than a norm for behaviour and are always susceptible to compromise. Only assimilated values are my personal values. Assimilated values reflect what is valuable to me. An assimilated personal value requires no choice on my part. When I want certain unassimilated values to become part of my value structure, I must exercise deliberation in following them until I am convinced of their value to me—then their observation will become spontaneous for me. For the expression of a value to become spontaneous for me, I must see its value in my personal life.

Paying lip service to obligatory values is no more useful than the chorus of parrots in a tree, who were singing out "Be careful of the hunter's net!" A wise old parrot had seen the hunter coming and had called out the warning. But the silly flock did not look at the ground to spot the hunter—to understand the fact of the situation—to establish a personal content for the words they had heard from the old bird. Instead, they continued to sit happily on the branches of the tree repeating the words which were empty of any real meaning for them: "Be careful of the hunter's net!" Even after the net had descended upon them, they wriggled and squirmed, caught in its web, screeching: "Be careful of the hunter's net!"

When I claim as my standards values in which I fail to see any personal gain for myself, I am in as risky a position, so far as expressing those values, as were the parrots in the tree, who mindlessly repeated the warning. Enjoined or obligatory values will become assimilated, personal values only when I see their value for me clearly and assimilate these values in terms of knowledge.

For the person with assimilated ethical values, life becomes very simple. No conflicts cloud his mind. For him, the teaching of Vedanta is like the meeting of gas and fire. Knowledge ignites in a flash.

2

HUMAN CAPITAL AND DEVELOPMENT
An Indian View

—S.S. GUPTA

I

In post Second World War period, two terms, 'Development' and 'Growth', have become very popular. They are economic terms but are being freely used by the common man. It is, therefore, desirable to know what they mean, at least for this article.

Economists tell us that all the countries of the world are not at the same level of material development. F. List, K. Marx, Rostow and others have given various stages of economic development. Efforts are being made in the under-developed countries to ensure that the country advances from lower stage of development to the higher level of material prosperity. This is termed as development. On the other hand, in developed countries efforts are being made to continue to advance to sustain the development already achieved. This is termed as 'Growth'. Thus the difference between Development and Growth is that of the stage of advancement and the problems faced by both are not the same. The process of development implies the change of a type of economy into some other more advanced type whereas the process of growth may not imply the change of the type of economy.

The concept of economic development originated from Europe. Physiocrats were the first exponent of it. Thereafter, Mercantilists gave it a great push and with Adam Smith and the industrial revolution, it got a tremendous momemtum. In this system economic consideration assumed overall control of all

Ex-Vice Chancellor, J-60, Janak Puri, Aligarh, 202001

human activities and even political and social systems became subordinate to it. The evils of the system, termed as capitalism, were soon felt and efforts have been made to correct the same. The moderates tried to control the evils through Labour Laws, Cooperative Movement and thereafter Mixed Economy. The extremists, not satisfied with this patch-work, tried to evolve a new socio-politico-economic system, termed as Socialism, where there will be no capitalism and no competition. But unfortunately, both capitalism and socialism have much in common. Both are materialistic concepts which believe in machines and technological development for more and more production at a faster rate. They think production is a barometer of development and human welfare and have tried to make man a machine and identify him as Human Capital.

The USA was discovered in 1756. It was a thinly populated country with a lot of natural resources. So in search to get rich quick, a lot of people from Western Europe migrated to the USA. In their zeal to get richer quickly, they tried to evolve a social system distinct from their parental society. They were uprooted from their homes and so had little respect for their churches, elders of their families, the society and the socio-political institutions. Their only motto and driving force was wealth and more wealth. At present the USA is at the top of affluent and developed societies and serves as a pole star for other countries.

A hurried review of this race for economic development gives us some important lessons:

The start of this economic development was with the inventions of small machines which slowly became bigger and bigger. They divided the country's population into 'haves' and 'have-nots'. The independent craftsman could not stand in competition with the mighty machines and was forced to seek employment in a factory. Class-conflict started. Hatred, jealousy, illwill became the dominant traits between the two warring groups, the exploiters and the exploited. This did not increase the total welfare of the population of the country as expected, but led to a situation which made the rich richer and the poor poorer. Misery increased.

Soon a stage was reached when developed countries could not sell their ever-increasing production within their own country markets. They could not even get raw materials in sufficient quantities. So, exploitation of backward countries started, first through international trade and thereafter in the form of imperialism and colonialism. The traits of exploitation, class war, hatred, jealousy, illwill, became internationalised.

A stage was reached when the thirst of the Capitalist World for markets and raw materials remained unquenched and the backward countries became slaves of developed countries. Map of the world had changed broadly into colonial powers and colonies. Competition, backed by military might, among the colonial powers to capture markets led to major world wars. The colonies have fast disappeared from the world map after World War II, but the exploitation of the weaker nations through unequal terms of trade continues even today.

The Socialist world also felt the necessity of getting markets in order to keep its countries on the path of the new paradise. They, in the new name of suzerainty, brought under the control of the big brother several other countries. Their conditions were no better than those of the slave countries of the Free World.

Pollock in his 'Economic and Social Consequences of Automation' has exploded the myth that technological development in the USA (and for that matter, in any other country) will not increase unemployment. The present times are living testimony to it. Even in the USSR this disguised unemployment could not be controlled and increased considerably. Certainly this cannot be termed development as a means for human welfare in either of the two systems.

Prof. Karl Mannheim in his 'Man and Society' has opined that this development with the help of technological development reduces average man's power to judge, decide and act for himself. To quote 'The fact that in a functionally rationalised society the thinking out of a complex series of actions is confined to a few organisers.... the average man's capacity for rational judgement steadily declines....' Is this development?

This craze of economic development is depriving workers, who are in majority in any society, of a sense of achievement and joy in their work. Gandhi wrote, 'I am afraid, by working with machines we have become machines ourselves, having lost all sense of art and hand work.' Earnest Hund has also remarked, 'We are witnessing an extraordinary development of power which tends to turn craftsmen into cogs in a soulless mechanism.' Is this development?

Machinery, which is an essential ingredient of economic development, undermines health as well.

Economic Development in its present form has resulted in the disintegration of families. Now even the nuclear family is breaking and there is no love lost even between parents and children. Worse still, there is no faith left. Husband doubts wife and vice-versa. Children have no faith in the parents and the mother has no time to spare for her children. Consequently, when the parents get old, children have no time and worse still, no real love for them. They are required to live in old homes and pay in advance for their graves.

Disintegration of families has also created a new problem. Now most of the crimes are committed in the super affluent society of the USA by teenagers. Problem children are becoming a major headache of the affluent society of America.

Fear, another by-product of economic development, is engulfing societies. Fear of automation, fear of TV, fear of Communism (God bless it has taken the back seat now under its own weight), fear of being left behind.... there seems to be no end of fears. What is life with fears can be anybody's guess.

Tensions and speed and more speed are destroying health and peace. Sleepless nights, headache, blood pressure, heart ailments, cancer, to count a few, have made life miserable.

In the name of development, we have interfered with nature in a mighty way. We have taken the path to conquer nature by mastering it, rather than by obeying it and in the process we have now got several types of imbalances—pollution of air, water, noise, and what not. We have invited distress and misery in a big way.

Psychologists tell us that every human being has primarily three instincts—acquisitive, possessive and competitive. It is these three instincts which are responsible for pressing for economic development. Out of these three, competitive instinct is aggressive in nature. This instinct, in order to minimise the fear of failure to acquire material progress and prosperity in ever increasing measure, takes recourse to cutting down costs and produce more and more in shorter time. So speed and more speed and ever increasing automation become essential. To serve this end, efforts are being made to change man also into Human Capital. Today, greater emphasis is being laid on development of Human Capital.

These three instincts develop 'I' (inflated ego) which teaches to differentiate and then to discriminate between 'I' and 'Others'.

Development of 'I' intensifies not only the three instincts of acquisition, possessiveness and competition but also gives three assumptions:

1. *Reality Assumption*: What he is and what the World is?
2. *Ideal (or value) Assumption*: What he should be and what the World should be?
3. *Possible Assumption*: What he could be and what the World could be?

A conflict among the various assumptions, sometimes conscious but often unconscious, leads to disintegration of human personality.

The concepts of Development or Growth, from an Indian point of view, have several shortcomings:

First, the term does not focus attention on the development of man, whose welfare, in fact, should have been the central point.

Second, the term refers to a single nation state and does not take a regional (South East Asia, Far East, Middle East, Asia, Europe etc.) or the world view of development. Even in one country development is not conceived to be uniform throughout the territory. There are more developed, less developed and backward areas in a country.

Thirdly, the term does not give any idea of the ultimate limit of the material progress. The limit seems to be the sky. But in the same breath, an economist tells us that the resources of a country are limited meaning thereby that there are limits to material progress. Thus, there seems to be an inbuilt contradiction. The economists try to explain it by saying that a country may have more technological development, greater speed and may exchange, beg, borrow or steal the resources of other countries to make itself richer. Thus, the concept seems to give birth to exploitation and even imperialism in different form—open or disguised.

Fourthly, the protagonists of this form of development do not bother to know how the economic development/growth of the country will affect a common man. If development/

growth mainly benefits the upper section of the society, making the rich richer, which is normally the case, what is the use of this development to the majority of the people of a country.

Fifthly, Gandhi and the Hindu philosophy tells us that man cannot be split into watertight compartments of an economic a social, a political, a legal or the like person. He is an integrated whole. In the present situation, development or growth takes care only of the material aspect of a country. This adversely affects man. This is apparent in the affluent societies where it is leading either to a lop-sided development of human personality or to a split personality. In either case, it is not conducive to human welfare or happiness. If people with material progress start suffering with headache, have to take sleeping pills to induce sleep, increasingly become a prey to diseases like blood pressure, heart ailments, cancer, etc. then it should not be called, in real sense, a development or growth.

Sixthly, these terms seem to spell out the aim of the material development. Marshall and Pigou tried to emphasise the objective of welfare. In course of time, it was found that it is an imperfect concept which can hardly be realised in real life. There appeared to be a conflict between individual welfare and general welfare. Then it was not possible to measure welfare and pronounce a judgement. And there was a faulty assumption that non-economic welfare remains constant. Robbins tried to skip over the whole problem of passing judgment or giving an aim. He took the posture of a scientist. Marx and other socialist thinkers talked about the aim of establishment of a socialist society which has turned out to be both unscientific and impractical. It had to leave in a hurry.

Human Capital

Economists tell us that man is the beginning and the end of all economic activities. So, the welfare of man is the primary concern of economics.

These economists have wrongly assumed a direct relationship

between man's welfare and his satisfaction of ever increasing material wants. Hence, emphasis, probably unknowingly, has shifted from man to ever increasing production and in the zeal to produce more, man has been reduced to the form of a Capital. The man to become an efficient Human Capital must be able to produce more and should become more skilful in his work. This means he must be more trained and more competent. He should work with speed and more speed. He gradually should become a machine and like a machine should become, with passage of time, technically more developed. Naturally, in this process the man's mental make-up, his emotions, his human values are asked to take the back seat. In other words, the difference between a living man and mechanic man, between a God and *Rakshas*, between an integrated man and disintegrated one, is overlooked.

Here a peculiar situation arises: Development or Growth means increasing country's production. And developing Human Capital also means increasing country's production with the help of this man by reducing him to the status of a soulless machine. Thus, man and his development are thrown to the background and the development or growth of the country takes the front seat.

II

Indian seers, who had their feet planted firmly on the ground opined that it is wrong to talk of development in relation to a country and of Human Capital as a means to country's ever increasing production. In their opinion development should refer to MAN not only as Human Capital but as an integrated personality including work skills and work habits. Thus the element of capital in human being is an inbuilt part of developed human personality.

In Indian philosophy, development means an all-round integrated and balanced development of man's personality. The seers believed that this developed human being will be an asset not only for oneself but also for others—country, world and the humanity.

Indian seers opined that a man has two dimensions—vertical and horizontal.

Vertical Dimension

In vertical dimension, a man has the following five sheaths:

1. *Material Sheath* (Ann Mai Kosh): Matter is essential and is at the lowest level. Body is made of matter. Permutation and combination of 125 elements (earth, water, air, fire, ether etc.) produce all types of bodies. Further to get this body going, matter in shape of food, air, water, etc. is needed. But there the importance or role of matter ends.
2. *Vital or Energy Sheath* (Pran Mai Kosh): Higher to matter sheath is energy sheath. Inside the body there is a subtle body which is functional. For example, there are five sense organs (ears, eyes, nose, tongue and skin); five organs of actions (hands, legs, speech, anus, sex organs); five breaths (breathing, excretion, digestion, blood circulation and nervous system); etc. These vital organs function with the help of some sort of energy, which is different from the energy of electricity, magnetism, light, heat, sound, etc.
3. *Manas Sheath* (Mano Mai Kosh): Higher to energy sheath is manas sheath. This deals with emotions. It is found in more developed form in human beings than in animals, birds or even plants. Western psychologists, at best call it conscious mind. It deals with desires (*Kama*) and actions (*Artha*).
4. *Intellectual Sheath* (Budhi Mai Kosh): This is higher to Manas Sheath. Western psychologists now admit that mind has three parts—conscious, subconscious and unconscious. The conscious part deals mainly with the outer environment and goes up to stage of learning and modern science. It is now an admitted fact that subconscious and unconscious mind are storehouse of innumerable unknown powers and if awakened like conscious mind can do wonders. For example, when one sleeps, with him conscious mind sleeps and sometimes subconscious mind awakens and appears in the form of dreams. Dozens of famous scientists—Watt, Iliya, Neils, Bohr, Henry Feher to name a few, admitted that they got solutions of their problems through dreams.
5. *Permanent Happiness Sheath* (Anand Mai Kosh): This is the highest sheath. Here, Indian seers opined, lives soul (*Atma*) which is a part of superconscious (*Paramatma*). They tell us that it is permanent and takes birth after death till it achieves salvation. Western scientists till recently did

not believe in the existence of soul and rebirth theory. But they are not that sure now. Through para-psychology researches they have found that when a person is mesmerised and is taken back to earlier lives, what he reveals of earlier lives has been found correct in many cases.

Horizontal Dimension

In horizontal dimension, man has the following:

1. *Family*—Presently they are breaking. There is neither integration nor development.
2. *Society*—Due to too much emphasis on matter, it is also getting loosely knit. The old cultural values are slowly being thrown in waste paper basket and the so-called modern values, which means westernised, are not being fully adopted. Mostly, the bad points are taken. The position has reached where one does not know even the names of next door neighbours, what to say of sharing their sorrows and happiness.
3. *World* (Humanity)—Due to rapid means of communication and material interests, world's boundaries have shrunk. But the fellow feelings and the humanitarian considerations have started taking a back seat.

The presentday development is eroding these three horizontal sectors.

Besides this, there are social, political, moral and economic aspects. Here too, in the name of development, only the economic aspect is getting the lion's share. The development is becoming lop-sided.

Indian seers felt that when we talk of development it should refer to man and not to a country and it should be all-round, integrated and balanced development. This means that man should develop vertically and also horizontally. When this is done, man will be happy, he will help others to be happy, the country will be better-off and humanity at large will be happy.

In such a development when the emphasis has shifted from a country to MAN, the difference between development and Human

Capital will automatically vanish and this new man will become not only a better capital but also a better human being. Due to his better qualities of head and heart and better self-control, almost all socio-politico-economic problems will automatically get settled at their respective places.

The aim of this development of human personality is *Anand*, i.e., bliss while living and Moksh (salvation from the bondage of birth and death) after death.

III

If we are interested in an all-round, integrated and balanced development or growth of man and not of an area of a country, or a whole country, or a group of countries, then it appears the Western approach of material development alone will have to be given up. In its place the alternative approach propounded by the Indian seers and which has, for centuries, proved its efficacy, will have to be followed. This approach will certainly integrate man vertically as well as horizontally and will lead him to the path of *Anand*. An outline is ventured here.

IV

Geeta is a world-renowned philosophical book which gives best jewels of the Hindu philosophy. In the battlefield of Kurukshetra, when the armies of *Kaurav* and *Pandav* had assembled and everyone was itching to test one's might, Arjun, a very renowned warrior, famous for his extraordinary excellence in archery (in modern terms, super Human Capital), requested Lord Krishna to take his chariot in the centre of the battlefield so that he may assess his enemies and evolve his strategy. When he reached the spot, he saw most of his dear and near ones in the opposite camp. He lost his integrated personality because suddenly he reached a dualistic situation—what to do and what not to do. This super Human Capital became diffident to fight. He asked Lord Krishna, why should he kill his dear and near ones? How will such a kingdom bring peace, prosperity and happiness to him? To his innumerable questions, Lord Krishna explained to him the theory of action (*Karma*). It is in this theory or *Karma Yoga*, or *Nishkam Karma* or stability of mind that we get answers to our present study. It helps, besides other things, in an all-round, integrated and balanced development of human personality. This integrated personality is key to *Anand*, i.e., bliss which should be the goal.

V

Indian seers, like Westerners, said that everyone has desires (KAMA). These desires may be economic or non-economic, or both. The satisfaction of these desires is desirable and, upto a minimum of bodily needs, essential. But which desire to select and in what quality is a million dollar question. This choice making in the Western terminology will depend upon the aim which one sets for oneself and the resources, including time, at one's disposal.

To satisfy desires (KAMA), one will have to act (ARTHA).

Newton, the great scientist, in his third law said that every action has a reaction in opposite direction. Our seers also opined that every action will have a result. They further said that good actions will have good results and bad actions will give bad results. Gandhi, in his inimitable style, provided logic to this statement by saying that if one sows *Babool* (acacia), one cannot expect to get mango fruits.

Indian seers were not enamoured by the Resultant Theory of the Westerners. In human actions, there is nothing like cancelling out bad deeds with good deeds. Here good actions will have good results and bad actions will have bad results and man will have to accept both. They will not be cancelled out with each other.

How much will be the time-interval between an action and its result? The Indian seers opined that the result of each action may be instantaneous or at a time-interval. When we throw a ball in the sky it is bound to return back to earth but when and where will depend upon a number of factors, viz., by which force was it thrown upwards, at what angle was it thrown, what was the gravitational pull at that point, what was the velocity and direction of the wind, etc. Similarly, the result of each human action will depend upon a number of factors. Due to these factors, the result may be immediate or after a time-interval. They felt that the time-interval may be so long as to pass on to the next birth. They believed in rebirth theory which now is being increasingly accepted by the Western world also.

Arjun, in the battlefield, in a dualistic mental state, asked Lord Krishna, why should he act? Why should he kill his near and dear ones? How will this give him pleasure (material) or happiness (*Anand*). Similarly, a common man will like to know why should one act?

Human body is made of matter. Again for its existence, it needs matter in the form of food. It has functional parts like heart, lungs, mind, eyes, etc. For their functioning it needs power or energy. This energy is generated by raw material of food consisting of vitamins, minerals, carbohydrates, etc. it has a *Manas* which is restless and always wants more and more and is never satisfied. It has a conscious mind to control *Manas* to rationalise wants. And it has subconscious and unconscious mind which, when awakened, seers tell us, can do wonders. And then there is spirit which, when goes out of body, makes it dead.

Lord Krishna and Indian seers tell us that one will have to act in order to satisfy one's body needs of food, cloth, shelter, education and various emotions. So, one, who is born, will have to act. There is no escape from it.

If every action is bound to give results then how to decide what to do and what not to do? How to have choice making? Lord Krishna provides two criteria of choice making. One of *Sva-Dharma* (one's own duty) and another of stability of mind (Sambhav or Sthiti-Pragya).

Indian seers opined that everyone is born with certain nature, i.e., characteristics. Some are born strong and some weak; some are born brave and some timid; some are jealous and some are kind-hearted; some are born with high degree of intelligence and some with low intelligence. The Indian seers also tell us, the nature of fire is to burn; that of wind to blow and that of water to flow. Similarly every human being must act as per one's nature. This is *Sva-Dharma* (modern science also now acknowledges Gene Theory).

After being born, one acquires certain traits from one's family, school, work-place, society, culture and social values. They also slowly take the form of *Sva-Dharma*.

Lord Krishna advised Arjun to act as per his natural instincts and also the acquired instincts, i.e., *Sva-Dharma*.

The second guiding principle to act is stability of mind (Sambhav). What is the meaning of stability of mind? How to acquire it?

When one is duty bound to act and there is no escape from

acting; when the result or consequences of each and every act will have to be borne; when the time-interval of the consequences of action is not known, it depends upon several factors and may go up to the next life; then rationality demands that one should act in a non-attached way, always trying to do good deeds.

Indian seers said that there are innumerable values but ten are most important ones. There ten values can be either positive or negative, they are:

	Positive	*Negative*
1.	Truth	Untruth
2.	Purity (Cleanliness)	Impurity (Pollution)
3.	Self-control	Indulgence
4.	Non-stealing	Stealing
5.	Patience	Impatience
6.	Forgiveness	Revenge
7.	Non-anger	Anger
8.	Knowledge of matter	Illiteracy
9.	Knowledge of soul	Ignorance
10.	Non-attachment	Attachment

As per the need of time and space new values can be added such as love, simplicity, non-violence, bread-labour, patriotism, piety (Karuna), etc.

If a person acquires negative values, because he is motivated by short-term selfish materialistic interests, he is bound to get attached and his actions are likely to go wrong or bad. By doing these actions, he will earn bad results and suffer. This is not rationality, conducive to his own happiness and also happiness or welfare of the society.

On the other hand, if one acquires positive values, like truth, self-control, non-stealing, patience, forgiveness, non-anger and knowledge of matter, one gets less and less governed by self-interest and material gains and so he is guided more and more by objectivity and rationality. This naturally implies good actions and consequently good results both for self and, still more important, for the society. This promotes happiness and bliss.

To act on the basis of positive values is to promote stability of mind.

There is no contradiction when one acts as per *Sva-Dharma* and stability of mind. Both are complementary and supplementary to each other.

When one acts with *Sva-Dharma* and stability of mind, then being non-attached and not motivated by unreasonable selfish interest, one acquires power of concentration. This power of concentration makes a man better worker, i.e., more efficient worker. These two traits also relieve tensions. Reduction in tension is conducive to better health. Better physical fitness means better efficiency.

Sva-Dharma, stability of mind and adoption of positive values should help in an all-round, integrated and balanced development of human personality. The man will get integrated both vertically and horizontally which will be helpful in establishing a better family, a better society, a better world order and a better socio-politico-economic order. This is the demand of the present times.

VI

It is very difficult to define the term value as different disciplines ascribe to it different meanings. For example, in economics, the term is used to denote the power of a commodity or service to satisfy a man's need. It is called 'Utility' and is used to determine the price of a commodity or service. Similarly, its meanings differ, when we talk of moral values, spiritual values and religious values.

The term is used in economics in a subjective sense. The value of a commodity or service differs with time, place and person. A rupee in the pocket of a rich person may not be so valuable to him as it may be in the pocket of a hungry man. Again, the utility, i.e., value of a banana to a person, who has already consumed six, may not be equal to the utility of the first banana which he consumed. It will therefore be a mistake to apply the same standard of valuation to different persons, places and at different times.

In spite of these difficulties, it is desirable to define the term. The word value is understood as desirable ideals and goals which are intrinsic in themselves and which, when achieved or attempted to be achieved, evoke a deep sense of fulfilment to one or many or all parts of what we consider to be the highest elements of our nature". Some thinkers consider value and principles as interchangeable words.

Prof. J.C. Kumarappa opined that values can be grouped into two main headings—self-centred and altruistic. When "we judge things in relation to ourselves we say it is self-centred and when measured against an external, or abstract ideal and in relation to others, it is said to be altruistic". But to lead to any degree of permanence it is necessary that the standard of value must be based on something apart from the person valuing, i.e., it should be altruistic.

In the West, two sets of values have been propounded. One set refers to happiness as an intrinsic value and the other set conceives right action as an intrinsic value. Some have tried to combine both.

M. Edgar Faure, Chairman, UNESCO, has put forward a comprehensive ideal and value namely 'to be'. Explaining the term, he said, 'that the aim of development is the complete fulfilment of man, in all the richness of his personality, the complexity of his terms of expression and his various commitments'.

Indian seers opined that social values or moral values can be taught but in order to imbibe them, one will have to practise them. One can learn in theory, the various processes of swimming or painting or dancing or singing. But one cannot become a swimmer, a painter, a dancer or a singer without practising them. So, one should not only know the meaning and theory of a value but should also imbibe it. 'Doing' is more important than 'knowing'.

Indian Rishis were of the opinion that knowing, learning and practising social values is not sufficient. One must have a faith in them. And the faith comes when one tests them through one's own experience.

It is desirable to identify the values, know their meaning, learn their theory and practise them in life. This will promote one's own happiness through development of an integrated personality and will have the widest possible influence on other peoples' lives. It will promote individual as well as general welfare together.

The learning and practising of various values will integrate a man and develop him. He will become a better man, incidentally also a better 'Human Capital' also. And at the same time, it will lead to a better development of a country, or a region and the world as a whole. There will be no conflict of interests and divergent pulls and pushes.

3

THE HUMAN VALUES
From Physical to Spiritual

—PROF. RAGHU NATH

From antiquity, scientists, philosophers and sages have investigated, theorized and written about the origin and nature of human beings. According to Darwin, the human being is nothing but an advanced species of the animal kingdom. According to Darwinian theory of "survival of the fittest", the basic human value is to fight with others for one's survival, i.e., live by the rules of the jungle. On the other extreme, sages of all ages have proclaimed the human being to be in the image of the Almighty. According to this perspective, the quest is to become one with the creator and his creation. Values embodied in this conception of the human being are those of oneness, togetherness and unity in diversity.

The purpose of this paper is to present a cosmology of human values that forms a hierarchy from physical to spiritual. We hope that such a cosmology would provide an integrated framework into which most of the prior work about human values can be fitted. We will also present a plan of action to move from physical to spiritual self. Cosmology without a plan of action is mere abstraction. On the other hand, a plan of action without underlying cosmology is rudderless and, therefore, ineffective. The ultimate quest is and should be to move from the physical level to a spiritual one. As human beings develop along the path from physical to spiritual self, they begin to live in harmony with nature, rather than destroy it.

The law of jungle would ultimately destroy not only other species but the very nature that sustains all species. Humankind,

Katz Graduate School of Business, University of Pittsburgh, Pittsburgh, PA15260, USA.

therefore, needs to move to higher values so as to rebuild and preserve the environment.

The Cosmology

The integrated framework comprises of seven stages of development from purely physical to spiritual. Each stage of development corresponds to a Chakra in the human body. These seven Chakras and their locations, as well as their esoteric functions are depicted in Figure 4.1.

We will now briefly describe each one of the seven chakras, its esoteric function, and values associated with it.

First Chakra—Base

The first chakra lies at the base of the spinal column. The area of the body it governs is the kidneys and the associated endocrine gland—adrenals. This chakra represents the primal life force. The basic values associated with this chakra are that of security and survival. These values are akin to the Darwinian theory of "survival of the fittest". Under the influence of this chakra, human behaviour is driven by the desire to survive, i.e., seeking food and shelter. When these survival needs are threatened, the human being resorts to fight syndrome leading to the destruction of other species and the environment.

Second Chakra—Sacral

This chakra governs the reproductive system. The endocrine gland associated with this chakra is gonads. The basic function of this chakra is sensation. In its positive form, it leads to pleasure and creativity. However, when distorted, it results in stimulation and possession. In the worst form, it results in seeking pleasure at the cost of others, i.e., resulting in sexual abuse and demeaning of others. At the best, it leads to reproduction and creation of new life.

Third Chakra—Solar Plexus

The areas of body governed by this chakra are stomach, liver, gall bladder, nervous system, and the endocrine associated with this

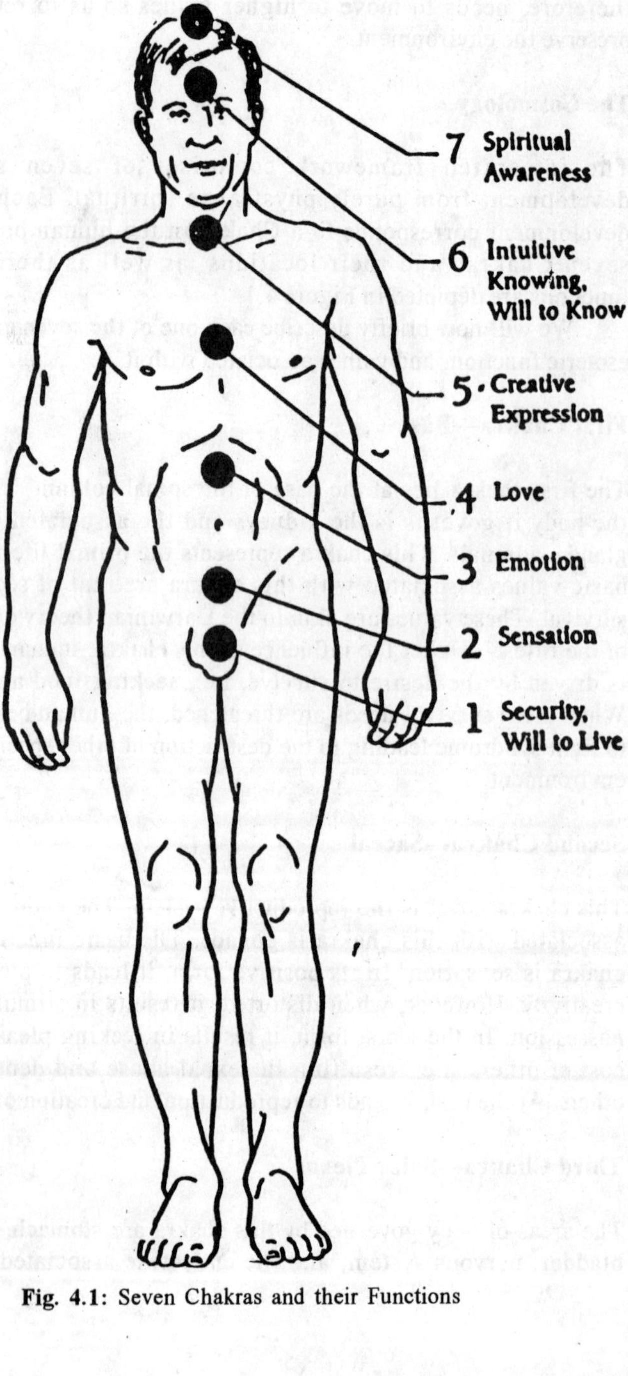

Fig. 4.1: Seven Chakras and their Functions

chakra is pencreas. The main function of this chakra is emotion. The underlying values are conditional giving, caring and compassion. When these values are distorted, they result in power over others and manipulative control.

Even, at its best, the giving and caring under the influence of this chakra is conditional. In other words, the person who gives expects something in return. It is a transaction in which the giving and receiving have to be balanced. Thus, the relationship developed under the influence of this chakra between two human beings is based on instrumental transactions. The prevailing theory of transaction costs fits well with this framework. When Bill Clinton talks about fair trade, he talks about the trade that is balanced between nations in terms of exports and imports. Notion of reciprocity among people and nations is consistent with this chakra.

First Three Chakras

The first three chakras are lower level chakras. They tend to satisfy the lower level needs of human beings as well as human groupings—ethnic or national. Whereas the first two chakras involve, primarily, physical forces, the third chakra involves feelings as well as thinking. Thus, both body and mind are involved in the affairs of the first three chakras. There is energy associated with these physical and mental forces. Thus, each of these chakras has its energy field. These energy fields continuously expand and contract reflecting one's daily experiences, feelings, and emotions. At the same time, there is a part of them that changes very little. Figure 4.2 presents a map of various energy fields.

Like a tree, each chakra has deep roots that appear physically to move or change only in very small increments over its lifetime. However, a tree's branches respond to every breeze, to changes of the seasons, to the movement of the sun across the sky, and even to the scurrying about of wild life in its branches. Similarly, a chakra, too, responds to many influences.

When the energy fields associated with the first three chakras are expanded more than the energy fields associated with the upper four chakras, balance of forces is tilted in favour of lower level needs thus resulting in survival, stimulation, possession and manipulative control. This not only creates disease (dis-ease) in the human system but disharmony and conflict among communities of

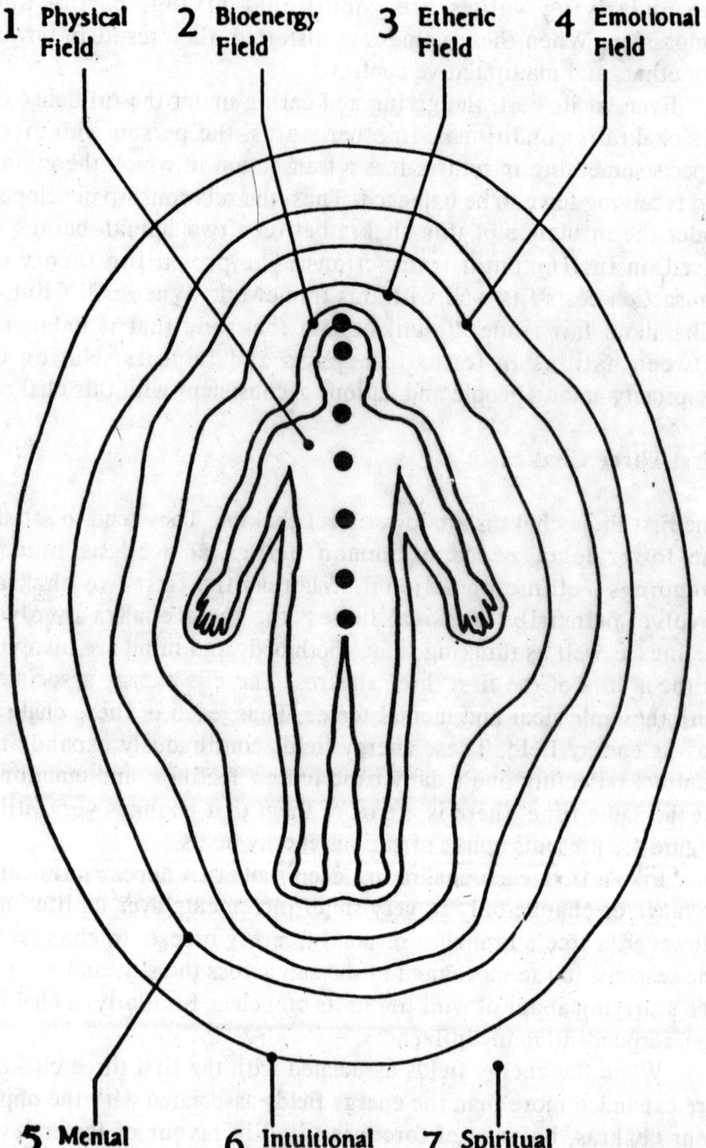

Fig. 4.2: Energy Fields Associated with Seven Chakras

people, i.e., the ethnic groups and the nations.

Fourth Chakra—Heart

The area of body governed by this chakra is that of heart, blood, vogus nerve and circulatory system. The endocrine gland associated with this chakra is thymus. The function of this chakra is love and the underlying values are those of unconditional giving, caring, and compassion.

In the scheme, this chakra is very crucial. Thus, when a human being advances from the third to the fourth chakra, a major transformation takes place. Due to this transformation, the human being transcends the lower level needs and develops the higher level values. Under the influence of the third chakra, giving and caring are conditional. But, under the influence of the fourth chakra, giving and caring becomes unconditional. The chain of reciprocity is broken. "Giving" becomes valued in itself without any desire for reciprocity. In other words, one becomes Christ-like. The peace and the bliss that results from such unconditional giving provides a reward of the highest order, much beyond the pleasure generated by receiving the favours from others in return.

In the fourth stage, the person experiences great change in the bioenergetic force field. Rather than the sensations and emotions experienced under the influence of the first three chakras, the desires die down, and peace and tranquallity prevails. Possessive tendencies give way to peaceful, loving energies. The system calms down. Fight and flight behaviour subsides. The stress experienced by the human system gives way to a feeling of calmness. This usually results in lower blood pressure, calming of nerves, as well as disappearance of other stress-related symptoms. This, in turn, releases a lot of positive energy in the human system which is then directed to unconditional giving.

Fifth Chakra—Throat

The area of the body governed by this chakra is bronchial and vocal chakra is lungs and elementary canal. The endocrine gland associated with this chakra is thyriod. The function of this chakra is creative expression. The underlying value is to create new and innovative forms and build new and creative things. These new forms may involve human habitats which are in harmony with nature. For example, it could be developing beautiful gardens, planting trees and creating other natural habitats. Self Realization Fellowship has developed several retreats. For example, the retreat at Encinita, California has a beautiful meditation garden. Wandering through this garden and meditating under its beautiful trees is, indeed, a heavenly experience.

in Pittsburgh, there is a confluence of three rivers. Looking at them from the top of Mt. Washington reminds one of the natural beauty the Lord created in this valley. In the years past when the rivers were clean, and the vegetation was green, this must have been a heavenly place. Propelled by the desire to conquer nature and satisfy our survival needs, we polluted the rivers, destroyed the natural vegetation and built factories which, for decades, polluted the air and created junk yards of rusting iron and scrap. The time has come for us to get back fo the higher level value of creative expression so that we can clean our rivers and restore the natural habitats.

Sixth Chakra—Head

Areas of the body governed by this chakra are lower brain, left eye, ears, nose, and nervous system. The endocrine gland is pituitary. The function of this chakra is intuitive knowing. The underlying value is seeking truth. The knowledge so gained gives the human being wisdom.

The most important thing that differentiates human beings from the animal kingdom is this quest for eternal truth. When this true knowledge is gained, one becomes Buddha—The Wise One.

The search for truth is the search for oneness, i.e., seeking and realizing unity in diversity. As Lord Krishna said to Arjuna, "Leave your desires behind. Come to me. When you thus surrender, you will become one with me. Then you will attain the Moksha."

Seventh Chakra—Crown

The area of the body governed by this chakra is the upper brain and right eye. The endocrine gland associated with this chakra is pineal. The function of this chakra is spiritual awareness. The underlying value is non-violence. As Gandhiji used to say, "Being non-violent is not akin to being passive. In fact, it is the most active state of existence one can imagine." In this stage, the need for aggression is gone. Instead, there is a reaching out to everyone and understanding all. There is a feeling of oneness and unity. All are treated with respect because everything is incarnation of the almighty. This includes humans, animal kingdom, and inanimate objects. It includes all and excludes none.

The seven chakras and values associated with them are summarized in Table 4.1.

TABLE 4.1: Seven Chakras and Their Associated Values

Chakra	Associated Values
1	Security, Survival
2	Stimulation, Pleasure, Possession
3	Conditional Giving, Caring, Manipulative Control
4	Unconditional Love, Giving, Caring, Empowerment
5	Creative Expression
6	Intuitive Knowing, Seeking Truth
7	Spritual Awareness, Oneness, Non-Violence, Peace

The Action Plan

In the framework described above, the seven chakras are in a hierarchy. The first three chakras are governed by lower level needs. Chakras 4 through 7 are associated higher level values. Whereas physical forces dominate lover chakras, spiritual forces are involved in the higher level chakras. Also associated with each chakras is an energy field. These energy (force) fields extend beyond the human body in concentric circles of increasing diameters. Each energy field has its unique frequency with which it resonates. Though these fields contract and expand daily, they also maintain a relatively constant relationship to each other over a long period of time. For example, Figure 4.3 provides Force Fields for two persons—A and B.

As can be seen from Figure 4.3, Chakra 1 energy field is expanded the most while Chakra 7 energy field is expanded the

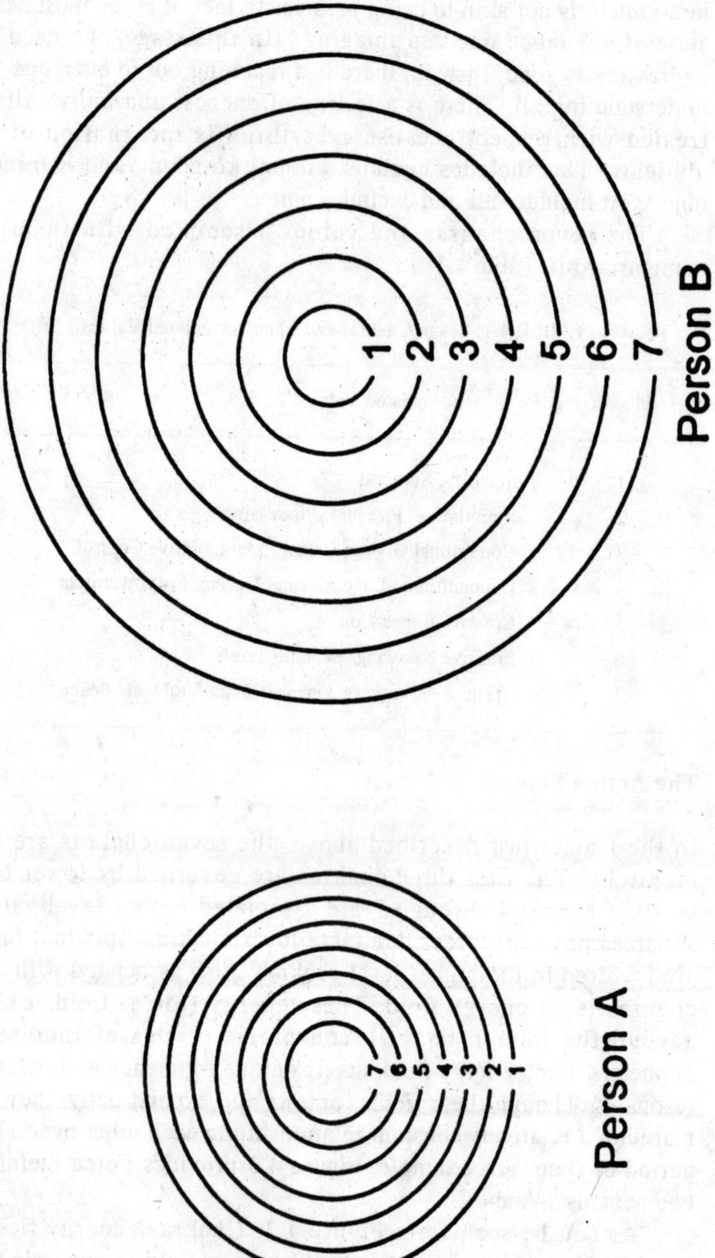

Fig. 4.3: Contrasting Energy Fields

least for Person A while the reverse is true for Person B. Also, overall, all the energy fields are expanded more for Person B than Person A. This implies that Person A values security and survival, while Person B is influenced by the spiritual values of oneness and non-violence. Thus, these two persons are at different stages of development. The path of development goes from the first chakra to the seventh chakra.

When a person is governed by higher order values associated with uper level chakras, these higher level values also influence the lower level chakras, thus, directing the energy of the lower level chakras towards positive aspects of the governing values. For example, when a person is influenced by the seventh chakra, the governing value of the first chakra becomes life force seeking security, but not at the expense of others.

Transformation Process

How does one move from lower level chakras to higher level chakras is the perennial question. The breakthrough or the transformation comes when one is able to move from conditional giving to unconditional giving. This breakthrough can best be achieved through the twin process of visualization and meditation.

Meditation

The path to meditation starts with learning pranayama, i.e., the art of deep breathing. There are many fine ways to the art of meditating properly. Learning how to meditate requires a guru or a teacher who can guide the learner through various stages of meditation. It is, therefore, highly recommended that those who want to pursue this development path must seek a "Guru" in whom they can put their trust.

Visualization

In addition to meditation, it is also important to learn the art of visualization. Again, there are a variety of ways of visualizing. It is beyond the scope of this article to describe all of these, and the seekers are encouraged to find teachers from whom they can learn the art of visualization.

Just as these two techniques can be applied at individual levels, action plans can be developed to implement higher level values through group, community and national action. For example, creating natural habitats, cleaning up the environment, replanting trees in a barren area, and other similar selfless acts are in congruence with the values of unconditional giving and creative expression which are associated with the fourth and fifth chakras. Thus, pursuit of these actions is in accordance with the higher order values.

Due to the pursuit of lower level values, communities as well as nations are being torn asunder. Recent racial riots in Los Angeles, ethnic cleansing in Bosnia, violence in India following the Ayodhya incident bear testimony to the destructive power of action that follows from the adherence to lower level values. There is a dire need to move to the spiritual values of oneness, unity in diversity, non-violence and peace associated with the sixth and seventh chakras.

Engaging in actions which are in accordance with higher level values will not only benefit communities and nations, but it will also bring joy and peace to those who are involved in these activities. It is, therefore, hoped that people in increasing numbers will dedicate themselves to actions which are congruent with the pursuit of higher level values.

REFERENCES

This articles draws extensively from the work of my friend, Leonard Laskow, M.D., who gave up his flourishing practice in Obsterics and Gynecoloy to experiment with a combination of visualization and meditation techniques to open the pathways to "Healing with Love". For a single source, therefore, I recommend:

Laskow, Leonard, M.D., 1992, *Healing with Love*, San Francisco, CA: Harper, San Francisco, A Division of Harper Collins Publishers.

For in-depth studies of the chakras, read:

Rendel, Peter, 1974. *Introduction to the Chakras*, New York, NY: Weiser.

Tansley, David, 1972. *Radionics and the Subtle Anatomy of Man*. Essex, England: Health Science Press.

4

EMERGENCE OF VALUES THROUGH HUMAN INTERACTIONS

—ASHWANI KUMAR

We all seek happiness. Yet it seems strange how after having taken the popular avenues to assumed happiness, one suddenly realises that the given or imagined goals have mostly been illusory. One finds oneself in a dilemma. Is it the nature of happiness to be illusory?

We all seek freedom—freedom from our economic limitations, freedom from physical and mental ailments developed mostly through our interactions with the physical and social environment. Yet one discovers that there is no escape from the interactions. Is the desire for freedom then a myth? Most of the traditional religious philosophies promise both happiness and freedom through the cultivation of a detached attitude towards life. But the human mind has been mostly failing in developing such an attitude for the last three thousand years, because the forces of life which have brought about self-awareness in human breast cannot be denied.

Pure Science, though a wonderful outcome of the human evolutionary mind, has been failing for the last half a millennium because it has always allowed itself to be sold to the world destroying forces of the greedy, competitive and aggressive technologies. Yet one is continually being led to the conviction that it is the higher technology that is always the victor in the final reckoning. The world continues to move further and further on the Juggernaut of soul-less technology towards its own annihilation.

One wonders whether there is yet an untried goal-less path walking along which one can experience happiness and whether

Ashwani Kumar, B-204, East of Kailash, New Delhi - 110065

there is a mode of interaction through such walking which can be continually liberating.

We are sensitive human beings because our universe has been working for billions of years bring about our sensitivities. Of course it is through human interactions with the external world that these sensitivities have come about.

One is aware that the theme is a challenge to our deeper inner selves—because we happen to be human beings and not beasts who don't feel the need to delve deep into their inner selves. Our capacity to think which distinguishes us from beasts raises a set of questions about the relevance of values for our lives, e.g.:

— What is a value?
— Why we value what we value?
— What is the significance of values in our interactions with the external world including other human beings?
— How a value affects the quality of our existence?
— Who is this valuer?

Many attempts have been made in the past to deal with such questions according to the local geographic and historic situations and levels, and all appear to be relative truths only.

Perhaps evolution is the only criterion by which the question of values can be meaningfully tackled. When we were evolving we had to compete with wild animals for survival. So there is an ancient deep layer of mind which is cruel, aggressive and selfish, very much unmindful of the right of other life-forms to co-exist. Slowly and gradually in time we observed that birds and animals loved their mate and offsprings as much as we love ours. We also observed that the local soils, birds and animals cooperated for mutual survival. Then our mental horizons began to expand to understand the participatory joys of living and the need for Truth. Beauty and Goodness in our conduct. This was the second, but very thin and fragile layer of our mind. Then there is a third layer of our mind which is confused because of the conflict in the two inner layers. This third layer is the space into which the noble layer of our mind is trying hard to unfold-only if we allow to unfold after the manner of the Cosmic unfolding from matter to spirit. Truthful, beautiful and noble minds keep springing up from time to time from the fissures in our earth to articulate the newer meanings of

Truth, Beauty and Goodness. Thus the Enlightened One says:

> "There is Truth in the stone, for the stone is here. But the stone has no consciousness.
> There is Truth in the plant and its life can expand; the plant grows and blossoms and bears fruit. Its beauty is marvellous, but it has very dim consciousness.
> There is Truth in the animal, it moves about, perceives sorroundings, it distinguishes and learns to choose, but it is not yet the consciousness of Truth. It is consciousness of the self only.
> The consciousness of the self dims the eyes of the mind-hides the Truth."
>
> —The Gospel of Buddha

Our Cosmos is a wonderful, kind and benevolent laboratory. Very patiently atom by atom, cell by cell it designs human body and evolves mind through body to project values which liberate our souls through participation in Her evolutionary processes. Perhaps it may not be out of place to recall the ecological values from the eco-philosophy of Dr. Henry Skolimowski. His ecological values of Reverence for all, Ecological Justice for all, and Frugality in our life styles stand firmly rooted in the participatory nature of human mind. It is the nature of the human consciousness to be creative and to expand holistically. Now creativity and holistic expansion of human consciousness are the terms that co-determine each other. It is through these two terms that our Cosmos expects us to proceed further. Therefore, one asks:

Can we, as human beings, conceive and identify ourselves with such values which are life-enhancing, not only outwardly but inwardly too? The question is multi-dimensional. In pragmatic terms, we are asking—

- — Can our technologies heal our Earth?
- — Can the searches of our biological sciences be directed towards understanding life without killing life?
- — Can our atmospheric sciences reorient their searches through communication with birds and animals?

— Can our social and religious institutions feeling the divine roots of human beings, lay greater emphasis on ameliorating the condition of the marginalised communities, downtrodden women in particular, instead of pampering those who are already rich and arrogantly wasteful?

— Can our art and literature be creative enough to project the newer truths of knowledge in the universe and newer beauties of human hearts?

In asking these questions we are asking ourselves

"Are we not what our values are?"

5

VALUES OF HIMALAYAN CULTURE

—M.L. DEWAN* AND VIR SINGH**

> Upon the tops of Mountains, the air being subtle and pure, we respire with great freedom, our bodies are more active, our minds more serene, our pleasures less ardent, and our passions much more moderate. Our meditations acquire a degree of sublimity from the grandeur of the objects around us.
>
> —J.J. Rousseau, 1970
> in "La Nouvelle Heloise"

Mountains are not just colossal masses of inert rocks. They are not simply remote, harsh and inaccessible. They are not only scenic, picturesque, full of breath-taking beauty, a paradise for tourists. Much more than their physical grandeur, they are the hospitable habitats of complex life processes, cradle of human civilization, an abode of cultural values.

Earth is a living planet, perhaps the only living planet in the cosmos. Life on Earth is the product of extremely complex natural processes. As a result of unceasing succession in nature, a myriad of life was created. Life was organised in ecosystems, species and genotypes. The whole myriad into this organisation has, more recently, been termed as biodiversity. Biodiversity, in essence, is the building block of life on Earth.

Ecosystem is a group of communities—of vegetation, of animals, of human beings-interacting with each other and their

* N-44, Panchshila Park, New Delhi - 110017

** Pant Nagar, Agricultural University, Hill Campus, Rani Chauri, 249199, Distt. Tehri Garwal, U.P.

physical factors. A population is a group of organisms of one species living in the same place at the same time. Birth, death, immigration and emigration are the factors contributing to the size of a population.

The community, a highly organised and stable group of populations, undergoes changes through a process called succession which is a process by which one community replaces another until a new, stable community is reached. Finally, the community reaches its last stage and remains the same for a long time. This final stage of succession is called the climax community. A climax community will remain stable until another environmental change occurs. Then the slow but orderly process by which one population replaces another repeats itself. An ecosystem, thus, is a community of living things plus all the physical factors that affect the community.

The different types of ecosystems are called biomes. A biome is made up of groups of similar climax communities that cover large areas of land.

Man, indeed, is a climax animal: more smart, more active, more dynamic, more adapted and, above all, more intelligent than all other animals created in nature.

Humanity started transforming itself into more developed hierarchical set-up-from individual into families, into populations, into communities, and, ultimately, into civilizations. It was the culture that shaped the human race, reshaped it into a variety of orderly organisations. Culture is the interwoven complex and fertile medium of human wisdom, insight, habits, behaviour, customs, creativity, innovations and numerous other virtues. Culture is a human interacting pattern with other human and non-human creatures and the physical envirionment. Culture teaches designing livelihood systems and living in harmony with nature and in peace and tranquillity with other fellow beings. Culture is a process which helps humans to manipulate, readjust, resynthesize, reshape and rebuild an environment conducive to further evolution of orders and values. It's a value-laden and a dynamic process. It is never static. Culture is, as it must be, a state that keeps humanity happy, peaceful and content and ensures a healthy, regenerative environment for all other non-human creatures. Civilization, in essence, is the environment of culture.

Culture is a manifestation of nature's diversity. Human is a product of nature and humanity has to depend for its sustenance solely on nature. There is no rule in nature for monoculture. As we see a myriad of biodiversity in nature, there is diversity in human cultures too.

Values of culture are shaped according to the specificity of an ecosystem. It is the pattern or orientation of diversity of an ecosystem-specific community, specific species and genotypes and specific environment—that determines human habits, primary, interacting patterns with ecosystem elements, ways and means of deriving energy and nutrients for sustenance and livelihoods.

Human values, they say, are created by soil and climate and man is what he eats. Soil and climate and food are specific to an ecosystem. Cultural diversity thus goes hand in hand with the ecosystem diversity. Ecosystem diversity is unique on Earth. And so is the cultural diversity.

The human cultural values are set not merely at individual, or family level, but, indeed, at community level. A community organisation is at ecosystem level. As variety of ecosystems makes up biomes, the cultural diversity is ultimately related to human civilization. If we are to realize a sustainable world, we must act at local level. Local level, in a sense, means ecosystem level. In the same way, to realise a sustainable society, we must begin to act at local community level.

Each culture, in fact, is a unique expression of a unique ecosystem. Thus each region is a unique ecocultural region. Each such region is a means for describing the distribution of animal and plant species as well as the human cultural values on the planet. If we could map all the ecosystems on Earth, we would easily come to understand the immense variety of cultures.

The Himalayan wildlands are important storehouses of the biological wealth. Intensive commercial, agricultural, industrial and urban settlements have led to alter the lowlands leaving the mountains perhaps the last stronghold of natural biodiversity.

The absolute number of species in the Himalaya may be less than in the lowland tropical rain forests, the mountain wildlands in general are the refuse for a great wealth of endemic and endangered species and communities.

The diversity-stocked Himalayan mountains are extremely inaccessible, harsh and, in many cases, very inhospitable for human beings. These landscape characteristics have helped the local inhabitats develop unique adaptive mechanisms. They have either transformed the local conditions partially (for instance, terracing of moutain slopes) or have adapted themselves to the conditions.

Himalayan heterogeneity, diversity, complexity and inaccessibility have given rise to hardworking people and decentralised local economics. Himalayan people are accustomed to fulfil their daily requirements from and create their economic framework in the surroundings environment. Thus they are fully equipped with the deep understanding of the nature-human relationship. They hold nature in great reverence.

The mountain people have rich extraordinary experiences than the plain people living in simple environments perhaps would never have. Their unique indigenous knowledge system has evolved on the foundation of social cohesion and ecological thinking. This knowledge system is highly dynamic, reflecting the scientific attitude of the society. In the wise and sustainable use of natural resources, the local people are highly innovative. They have developed innovative farming systems, farming situations, cropping systems, food-producing technologies and diversified economics—all linked with culture and history. Geographical and ecological opportunities and constraints (e.g. location, climate, soil, local plants, and animals) are reflected in local culture. Mountain farmers' values, knowledge, skills, technologies and institutions have been the factors influencing the type of agriculture and innovations, of consciously and skilfully manipulating the bio-physical and socio-economic resource base and judiciously harnessing the outcome of ecological processes.

Limited accessibility in the Himalayan mountains keeps the community-based culture alive. This is the most desirable value of the culture helping maintain the social cohesion intact and strong. This, indeed, should be regarded as a life-line for any local culture. Common history, wisdom, experiences and common control over Common Property Resources (CPRs) are the various integrating factors of mountain culture. The community-based culture is often reflected in sharing or exchanging germsplasm, labour, farm products, agricultural implements, draught animals and in community agricultural operations and irrigation. The communities have designed various measures to protect, preserve and conserve their natural resources and environment. Mass movements for safeguarding CPRs, e.g., Garhwal Himalaya's oft-quoted Chipko Movement, Anti-Tehri Dam Movement and Save Seeds Movement are the remarkable cultural response against the external forces detrimental to the local culture.

Local decentralised economy of the Himalayan mountains also gives rise to austerity in culture which directs people extract from the nature not beyond the threshold level of requirement and get satisfied with the minimum. This also creates sensitivity for the welfare of community as well as all other non-human forms of life.

Himalaya has entered the inner core of humanity perhaps since the very dawn of human awareness. All the major and minor religions render Himalayan mountains spiritually significant and the most sacred place on Earth. Himalaya is variously known as Nagadhiraj (the king of the mountains), abode of Gods, Paradise on Earth, place of pilgrimage, etc.

Lord Krishna in the Bhagwat Gita identifies Himself by saying, 'among steadfast I am Himalaya'. Great Sanskrit poet Kalidasa refers to Himalaya as 'yardstick to measure the Earth'. In his *Kumarasambhava*, Kalidasa describes how the union between Himalayan and a female mountain produces a daughter, destined to rid the world of evil. *Skandapurana* says, 'as the dew is dried up in the morning sun, so are the mankind's sins at the sight of the Himalaya'.

Sacred Hamalayan mountains are the places of ceremonial sacrifice and destinations of pilgrimage. Buddhists and Hindus make a strenuous pilgrimage to Mount Kailash to acquire merit for rebirth and salvation. Kailash is home of Lord Shiva and eternal resting place of Mitarepa and five hundred Buddhist saints who have attained nirvana. Nanda Devi, goddess of bliss, is assumed to reside on the peak in the Kumaun Himalaya named after her. The height of the mountains has divine significance and all high peaks are considered suitable locations for temples. The people visit these temples to seek blessings from the deities who reside there.

In the words of great eco-philosopher of our times, Professor Henryk Skolimowski: "Like no other mountains on this Earth, the Himalaya belongs to all humanity. Each of us has been personally tied to the Himalaya. For who of us has not dreamt about going there, and being there-if only for a while? Who of us has not been dazzled by their beauty and radiance? Who of us has not been inspired and humbled by the Himalayan ethos—so overwhelming, so much beyond us, and so much calling us to measure ourselves against us."

Garhwal part of the Himalaya was formally known as Kedarkhand. It was here that Shiva was traditionally worshipped. There are also strong suggestions of Buddhism and Jainism; the *Siddh* and *Nath* cult and *Naga* worship have had their days here. With the consecration of the Badrinath temple in the 9th century AD, Vishnu worship gained the foothold. It is generally accepted that Shankaracharya (AD 788-820), a Namboodri Brahmin from Kerala and a great social reformer, established the Vishnu image at Badrinath AD 815-20. He died at Kedarnath in AD 820, where his *Samadhi* (final resting place) is located, a befitting memorial to one who revitalized the Hindu faith all over the country.

Accomplishing the four dhamas (sacred places of pilgrimage) in Garhwal—Gangotri, Yamunotri, Kedarnath and Badrinath—is regarded to be a complete and final pilgrimage, ensuring *moksha* (salvation) for the devout pilgrim.

Himalaya is a big force which unites humanity. Himalaya is the meeting point of four big cultures. In the far north is the Tibetan (Lamaist) culture, which is the cold desert and foot of high peaks like Everest. The Islamic culture, which developed with contacts with Middle East and West Asia, is in the Hindukush. The Indic culture' hill edition which extends from Kashmir to Bhutan and Aranya (forest) tribal culture in Arunachal Pradesh, extending in the South-East Asian hill. These all were united by the human qualities of courage, hard work and adventure, which are the unique gifts of the Himalayan environment.

All cultures dwelling in the Himalaya, especially the Hindus and the Buddhists, the two major religions, have been cultivating the spiritualism.

This sanctity of the ecosystem (they are part of) instills in them a sense of reverence for the whole life, a sense of care for their environment. This generates a sensitivity in the minds of the people. This makes them creative and dynamic. This makes them conservation-conscious. Sacred mountains, sacred rivers, sacred groves, sacred seeds, sacred trees have been the cultural means for healing the Earth, for healing themselves.

Whether in art, literature or religion, mountains provide powerful symbols of spiritualism. People have attempted to portray their revelations by using mountain imagery in literature and art to evoke the sacred and instill a deeper meaning to ordinary aspects of life.

The Vedas (the books of knowledge of the Aryans) were composed in Garhwal Himalaya and they make telltale references to various geographical features of this region. The practice of horoscopy and astrology, offshoots of Vedic knowledge, flourished, and Deoprayag located on the banks of Alaknanda, a major tributary of Ganga, remains an important centre for the production of astrological charts and calendars. The environmental purity coupled with the sacredness of the Himalaya is a tonic for creativity and bringing out the best forms of art, literature and philosophy adding new values to the culture. The environmental purity of the sacred mountains has raised the mental status of the people very high. Their contribution to the human civilization is enormous.

The Mountain Agenda, presented at the UNCED in Rio de Janiero in 1992, also recognises the values of sacredness: "Cultivating the sacred or spiritual is crucial in evoking the respect for mountain environments and is necessary to lead to more concerted efforts in restoring the perilous ecological balance of mountain regions in the wake of increasing population and land-use pressures: it is also crucial for reawakening respect for mountain people."

As the urban-industrial-technological trap is becoming rampant, a common culture, or a mainstream culture is bringing the whole world under its umbrella. Ecological and social thinker Raymond F. Dasmann refers to this culture as "biosphere culture". Says Dasmann, "The new technological society has now become a global phenomenon, blotting out formerly self-reliant cultures and essentially assigning to all people a role in the new economic order."

The new global technology is engaged at the present time in what amounts to war against the natural resources, i.e., the fundamental building blocks of life and the local or ecosystem cultures, like that of Himalaya, are falling prey to the biosphere culture. Emerging from the dominant culture is the new economism based on false accounting. The noted eco-philosopher Henryk Skolimowski questions and opposes the new economism because, "it impoverishes us as individual existential beings, cheapens us with regard to what we can become, it robs us of our spiritual heritage.... It should be questioned and opposed on ecological grounds...."

The world being brought under one umbrella of new economic

order, of new biosphere culture cannot be the real world. Nor the notion of 'a global village' signifies a happy, content world. The divine reality is this that the world is diverse, colourful, heterogenous and much more than can be conjurèd by human imagination. Every thing is connected with every thing else in the cosmos. The ecosystems, the species, the genotypes and the environments on our living Earth, in spite of having their own existence, are linked with each other. The complex intra- and inter-relationships ensure eternal existence and service for each life form. Despite this diversity, the living world is a unitary whole. This is unity in diversity. Unity in uniformity, as a law of nature, is non-existent. It may be only a theoretical notion. The new economism must be cursed and opposed, for it leads to the creation of a uniform world.

Man is only one of the countless species on Earth. If the whole planet turns into the monoculture of human beings, it will, without a shadow of doubt, become "lifeless". In order to sustain, man has to live in dynamic relationship with all other things-living as well as non-living. Devoid of this, he cannot exist for a long time. The biosphere culture led by new economism threatens human life in two ways: it regards the planet as belonging to only the human beings and derecognises the existence of other forms of life; secondly, it deteriorates the very environment in which humans have to live, survive and regenerate. The biosphere culture, unquestionably, is valueless.

The ecosystem (local) cultures seek to establish viable relationship between human beings and non-human creatures and environments and are pregnant with aesthetic values of reverence for life. The greatest challenge before mankind today, therefore, is to save the ecosystem cultures from being eclipsed by the demonic biosphere culture.

To save, regenerate and preserve the ecosystem, eco-regional or bioregional cultures, the key response has come up in the form of bioregionalism. Faced with the declining ability of the Earth to support life and the possible extinction of our own species, bioregionalists have long realized that a key part of our relations with nature is repairing-wherever possible—the damage done to natural systems, and recreating human cultures capable of flourishing in an ecologically sustainable manner through time.

Himalaya is the most glorious part of the Earth. And so is its culture. Himalaya is the most precious and valuable heritage of the Earth, and its culture that of humanity. If Himalaya be considered as yardstick to measure Earth, its culture should be a scale to measure the humanity.

We remind the readers of the words of the celebrated eco-philosopher Henryk Skolimowski which further infuse the glory of the Himalaya in our minds:

> Keep your gaze fixed on the Himalayas and
> all your little worries will melt away.
> Keep your gaze fixed on the Himalayas
> and you will bathe in beauty.
> Keep your gaze fixed on the Himalayas
> and you will be closer to Gods.
> Keep your gaze fixed on the Himalayas
> and you will be closer to your inner self.
> The Himalayas are a symbol of
> our potential greatness and godliness.
> They are also a very potent symbol
> of our times. So many past religious
> symbols have crumbled, as they are
> unable to sustain us any more. The
> Himalayas stand undiminished.
> They unite people of all religious
> denominations. They are one stupendous
> altar at which the earth sings the
> glory of creation. When you are close to
> Himalayas, you can hear their peaks singing
> amidst the total silence.

We conclude by quoting from the article "Envisioning a Sacred Himalayas for a Sustainable Society" by one of the authors (M.L. Dewan) which sumarizes one aspect of the story of Human Values.

> Bless that Mother Nature be kind to us
> The Heavens give us peace
> The Earth be Gentle
> Gentle be the waters that flow,
> Gentle be the plants and herbs that grow.

May the past be kind,
the future benign.

—Atharva Veda 19.9.1

Drawing inspiration from this verse from the Atharva Veda and taking into account the realities of the modern Himalayas and India, our attention has to be directed to four aspects:

- The resources of the Himalayas should be preserved, developed and efficiently utilised for the benefit of the people. At present, its resources are being mis-utilised and will in the future take us to the path of non-sustainability.
- The Himalayan communities including the children, the women, youth and all members of the society have to develop a spark of awareness in themselves. This spark has to stem from an awareness that we are the custodians of the Holy Himalayas—the land of ages and sages, the land of perennial and ageless wisdom, which fertilises and irrigates a major portion of the Indian sub-continent. If the Himalayan region decays, India decays. At present, these communities are migrating, especially the adult male population, to the plains and cities because the natural resources are lying unutilised, underutilized or are being mis-utilised. There is enough potential in these resources of land, water, forests, grassland, cattle, medicinal plants, etc. which could support the present population and ensure an adequate quality of life. The communities simply need education and training and a spirit of adventure, sacrifice as well as partiotism. The Himalayas have been a source of inspiration for so many generations. What is now happening to the inhabitants of Himalayan region has to be reversed with building up of self-reliance and self-esteem among these communities.
- Non-polluting small-scale industries starting with agro-based resources such as horticulture, fruits and nuts, sericulture, apiculture, mushroom culture and dozens of other enterprises have to be developed and/or revived.
- Environment-friendly tourism has to be promoted for not only seeing the various places and origin of river systems,

glaciers and snow-clad mountains but also for drawing inspiration from them. We can have religious tourism, or the human-value-promotional kind of tourism, and in many cases think of developing what is now called Ancient Futures-in other words, learning from the past what has been good in our culture, civilisation and environment.

6

LIVING VALUES FOR A VALUED LIFE

—JUANITA SKOLIMOWSKI

Who Am I? Among the most important questions a young person struggles with are "Who am I?" "What is my role in this world I have been born into?" This alone is a significant assignment to accomplish over the years of maturing.

You can be a gift to the world by coming to know yourself, your core values; and by living these values to enhance the world. It may not seen clear yet, but the world needs your good living values.

The Greek philosopher, Socrates, said: "an unexamined life is not worth living." Coming to know what you value is most important for a fulfilled life. Knowing and choosing right values makes for a valued life. To know who you are is to know your values.

What are Values? Understanding values can be difficult because they are not clearly seen at first. But values are very real—as real as the air we breathe. There are many values in the world. Some are like fool's gold. They are enticing, beautiful but they are not true gold and thus cannot enhance your life. Others are true gold because they lead to a more enhanced and meaningful life.

At the core of every action is a value. Any action is based on some value, some purpose. For instance, you eat food because you value good health and living. You meet people because you hope to make friends—you value friendship.

Many times people are not aware of the values that underlie their living. They just do things a certain way. By knowing what you treasure and then acting with that in mind, you are living your values.

Where Do We Get Values From? In coming to know "who you

Sienna 89 M39, 00-815, Warsaw, Poland.

are", you must start with your own roots. These roots are your family, culture, and all past experiences up to now. These have shaped who you think you are and how you see yourself and others.

We learn our family's values by absorbing them from our family. The family is a primary teacher of values. As children we simply absorb values. A family's way of living is being passed on from one generation to the next. Some of the underlying values are articulated as "our values". But mostly children imitate their parents actions and may not even know that a given value was absorbed into their identity. As emerging adults, you can begin to trace the values you have ingested from you family. It is the beginning of the process in finding "who you really are".

Culture imbues values through larger institutions such as the community, school and religion. These values are strongly promoted as values to live by all. They help to promote a commonality in identity as well as action which thereby promotes order, cohesion, and common purpose. Often these values promote a standard by which to measure oneself and to live by. None of us can possibly live all of these cultural values and so we choose those that we really value. Culture is a very powerful teacher of institutional values. Everybody acquires a part of his or her identity being shaped by these values.

Another important source of values is our past experience. you not only acquire values through experience, but you use experience for testing values which are held subconsciously. Be aware of the nature of your experience. Be aware of the nature of your subconscious values. Be aware how the two meet and how they reflect on each other—because experience illumines your values but values also illumine the nature of your experience. It is a subtle and deep dance of which you want to be aware.

How Do Values Guide or Limit Us? The way we live and act reflect our values. We can either live our values by choice or we can stumble gropingly being led and misled by them. If you live and act mindlessly, that is without introspection, then you live an unexamined life. You are like a boat in the water with no rudder. You are going but who knows where.

Values are always there behind your actions. Most people are unaware they are living their values by their actions. It is this unawareness that is often at the root of confusion and darkness. When we are aware of our values, they guide us on the path of light and coherence.

How Can I Begin to See the Values I Live? To begin to see values is a painstaking process. One first learns by experience what works and what does not. It is like the time when you were a baby and you decided to walk. You pulled yourself up to a chair or someone's leg and then tried to take a step. And you fell down. But you wanted to walk. So you tried and tried until you could. This is how you will learn about values and learn to be an adult, responsible for yourself and to life. It may seem like a difficult process. If you think it is a difficult process, be assured it is difficult process. Everybody has gone through this difficult process and you can and will do it as well.

How Do I Practise Choosing Right Values? Begin with Yourself.

Be Watchful of Your Actions. Try to observe with compassion, detachment and understanding—yourself and others. Find a special time and place, perhaps once a week, to reflect over the actions of the week which you think were significant.

Ask Yourself These Questions:

— What were the values behind my actions and behaviour?
— How did it feel? Did it feel right? Why? Did it not feel right? Why?
— Did it bring well-being to me or others? Why?

From repeated actions that you observe, you will begin to see a pattern. Perhaps you will decide to keep a journal as your companion. The patterns that emerge are the circumstances of actions done over and again. Thus, you can identify the pattern by looking at the picture around the action—who, what, when, and where. From observing the pattern, you will begin to see the value behind the action.

If you continue to observe these "scene", you will see that there are consequences to every action. Each action has a value or intention within it and each action leads to a consequence. Now look at the consequences of your actions—some you may like and others you may not. If you don't like the consequences, don't be furious with the consequences. You simply have to go deeper to the values that brought the consequences you didn't like. At this point you might want to enter into dialogue with the values that brought you to grief.

Thus you have arrived at a new understanding—namely that you can choose and change values as you come to see and comprehend them. All people struggle with their values. Many have been able to change their values so that from these values follow actions which they consider right and appropriate. You can do this too.

Practise this process of indentifying and choosing the right values for yourself. Remember to value yourself. Remember that the person who cares to examine his or her values and choose them carefully is a beautiful person. For this is a courageous process. Be patient in your development and have faith in yourself. And learn to appreciate your own creativity in living and expressing your life.

Suggestions for Choosing Right Values. A good value means a sense of integrity or wholeness within yourself. It feels right inside—you appreciate yourself for those actions that express that value. Right living means living in integrity with yourself. Use your conscience as your guide in choosing and living right values. If you do some things in which the consequences don't feel good inside, don't do them. You are harming yourself and perhaps others by that action.

A good value in action brings well-being to others and yourself. It might be an action which helps the environment. It might be an act of kindness to some person or creature in need. It could also be refraining from a negative reaction to a negative action by another.

Summary of Living a Valued Life

- By knowing your values, you can choose right living.
- Responsible action is a result of knowing one's values.
- All actions have values.
- You can choose the values to live by.
- What you value is what you treasure. Look at what you treasure to identify your values.
- Some values bring integrity, contentment and happiness; other values bring confusion, strife and unhappiness.
- The ability to see the deeper values is the key to your good choices.
- Understanding one's values helps one live a valued life.

7

THE HIGH ROAD

—HENRYK SKOLIMOWSKI

I

What are values? Commands from heaven. Even if they were not, they should be treated as such. Whose heaven? Our joint common heaven: the world conceived of as a place of peace, justice, dignity, beauty and happiness.

Pigs do not need values. Neither do we—if we agree to live in a pigstay. Criminals, pathological killers and people without any sense of good and evil do not need values—as they live mindlessly and sometimes kill others mindlessly.

Only we need values, we the human beings who uphold a sense of sanctity of life, who believe in the beauty and dignity of life, and who aspire to make life beautiful and dignified. Values were thus, invented for those who have high regard for life, who, in a sense, conceive of life as a gift of heaven. In this sense values are commands from heaven—attributes of our thinking and behaviour which bring us closer to heaven.

On one point there can be no disagreement: values are these vehicles, these modes of our being and forms of behaviour which make us supremely human; not just ordinarily human. For our ordinary humanity so easily slides into a behaviour characteristic of the pigstay. *Only when we try to be supremely human, we become human*. Such is our predicament—and such is our road.

The problem with values—religious, ethical, social, existential—begins when we start to articulate the idea of heaven, the idea of the human, the idea of justice, dignity, sanctity of life.

Sienna 89 M39, 00-815 Warsaw, Poland.

Although the interpretations of these ideas are many, and sometimes they clash with each other, this should not prevent us from pursuing the High Road of our humanity.

To sceptics and cynics, we shall respond from the outset: no, it is not the case that everything is relative. There is a life of dignity, beauty, justice and freedom, on the one hand, and there is humdrum, undisciplined, sloppy, irresponsible existence, on the other hand. The former requires high values and is an embodiment of high values. The latter is a renunciation of high values—as it represents this variant of the human condition which is much below our possibilities. So the discourse on values begins with the question: what kind of human do you want to be and do you think you deserve to be?

The literature on the subject of values is enormous. It is expressed in religious books, in philosophical treatises, in dramas and novels, in essays and editorials. Almost everybody is vying for your soul. Yes, *to influence and control your values is to possess your soul.* Beware of that.

In the West the most articulate positions on the subject of values are expressed in books on ethics, such as *Nichomachean Ethics*, by Aristotle, or *Ethics*, by Spinoza. They are the treatises showing us the High Road. Much can be learnt about human nature by studying these treatises.

In India the most valuable discourses on values can be found in such sacred traditional books as the *Upanishads* and *Bhagavad Gita*. These books are still the source of moral guidance in people's lives. Again, these books outline the High Road of humanity.

The old venerable books on values give us a map of how human beings have struggled with their own nature and their own destiny. Yet with each new epoch, new problems arise and new threats appear to our integrity, to our quest for beauty, to our striving for dignity and divinity. In our times the threats to our identity, to our dignity, to our well being have been numerous. We need to recognize them and find appropriate moral responses. For if we don't, we drift; and end up in confusion, incoherence and meaninglessness. We abandon the High Road for a confusing one. The older moral and ethical strategies for safeguarding our integrity are still valid in many ways. However in our times new moral insights and strategies must be found to cope with new threats. Of these new insights I will concentrate on the following three:

1. Don't be too easily persuaded that you amount to nothing. You are a glorious star of God's horizon.
2. Don't allow yourself to be easily manipulated for the benefit of some and at the expense of many others. Your quest is one of universal justice and fairness.
3. Don't allow yourself to be used for the schemes which work to the detriment of other humans, of non-human beings, and of nature. Your duty is to encourage and enhance inter-species solidarity and the well being of all beings.

The above precepts follow from one idea of the sanctity of life. You need to remember: if sanctity of life is not upheld, only chaos, confusion and disintegration can result.

II

You may now wonder why do we witness many new threats to human dignity and human sovereignty in the world, which, we were told, was becoming more and more civilized? Perhaps we should make a clarification by noticing that the ever-growing development of civilization does not make society ever-more civilized. Something has happened in the way our civilization has developed. The promise of the civilized life in the wake of powerful forces of civilization has not been fulfilled. On the contrary, by some kind of strange dialectics, the powerful unfolding of civilization has unleashed great forces of savagery.

The individual has been caught in the web of the powerful forces which civilization has developed. Science and technology at one time promised to be the liberators of humankind. Through their benefits, universal fulfilment and happiness were to encircle the earth. This has not happened. Instead the more powerful science and technology has become, the more clearly they attempted to subdue the individual to their cold rational schemes. The great philosopher Immanuel Kant (1728-1804) already perceived this danger as he saw that science was good at exploring the external world but mute about human freedom and human dignity. He, therefore, declared: "The starry heaven upon you and the moral law within you." This was a radical separation of science from morality. It was an explicit assertion that the laws of science govern the outside universe, while the moral universe of the human is governed by the inner imperative of human conscience. Hence "the moral law within you". Freedom and sovereignty of the individual are rooted in the moral conscience of the humans, which is outside the domain of science. Hence the conclusion: science must not meddle in our moral universe. We are the moral sovereigns upon ourselves.

The salutary teaching of Kant is still relevant for our times, particularly as science and technology, if only indirectly, have attempted to subdue and manipulate the human universe to the imperatives and schemes which have very little to do with human happiness and liberation; and have much to do with greed profit, expansion, control and manipulation. In these schemes of control and manipulation, the individual is so often reduced to a pawn, to a cipher, to a nothing. As the result of the unrestrained reign of science and technology, we have witnessed a thoroughgoing process of *reduction* of the human to cogs and wheels, whereby the individual is deprived of freedom, dignity and sovereignty.

Thus it is extremely important for you personally not to be too easily persuaded that you amount to nothing. You are a very wonderful creation of the universe. Thus fight for your dignity, freedom and sovereignty. There have always been forces in the human society which attempted to level down the individual. But these forces have never been so numerous and so powerful as in the technological society.

The second precept which I stated was as follows: don't allow yourself to be manipulated for the benefit of the powerful rich and at the expense of the dispossessed poor. The difference in status, power and wealth has always been a fact of life. But nowadays we confront a new phenomenon. After centuries and millennia of the gradual disappearance of outragious inequities, during which we have consciously and deliberately promoted equity and justice among people—we are now witnessing sinister attempts to reverse this historical process. Through some clever, if not diabolical schemes, during the last decades or so, the rich have become richer and the poor poorer. This is most strange and unjust. This, in fact, flies into the face of the idea of justice, morality, humanity. As this gap between the rich and the poor increases, we observe great suffering and anguish. The progress of the rich is marked by the blood of the poor. This whole new development is unholy, immoral and it must be resisted. Otherwise, the growing process of injustice will result in the blow-up of the poor. The five per cent of the privileged ones cannot be the rulers of the planet. For this is against democracy, against justice, against God's plan.

The third precept which I stated asserted: don't allow yourself to be used for the destruction of nature. Don't align yourself with any schemes or practices which lead to the needless destruction of the fragile cycles of nature. Let us be aware, we have always harvested and used nature to our advantage. What we have witnessed in our times is the wholesale destruction of nature; also the accelerated destruction of species. Remember, once you eliminate a given species, even God cannot return it back to existence.

The protection of nature—as our Mother, as our habitat, as our sustenance—is enormously important, and it is now our new moral imperative. In olden days people lived in natural harmony with nature, woven into its cycles. There was no need to exhort humans to protect nature for it was their outer skin, so close to them that they would not dream of mutilating it. Besides, they had not the means to do so.

Then the humans separated themselves from nature and sought their freedom through subduing nature and through the manipulation of the external world. The exploitation of nature—to man's advantage and the manipulation and control of the external world became the *unwritten moral commandments of the post-Renaissance man.* These commandments have become ingrained on the technological consciousness of 20th century people. The grip of these commandments is still powerful, in spite of the fact that we now clearly see what havoc we have brought upon nature. It is thus important to announce the protection of nature as our new moral imperative.

The main conclusions of our discourse, so far, are as follows:

— resist reduction of your humanity to the stuff of the machine;
— resist the spread of injustice-remembering that we are one human family, united by the bond of solidarity;
— resist the destruction of nature-remembering that you are one of its branches.

The problems I have discussed are not typical moral problems which one finds in traditional books and precepts. Rather they are new moral problems of our times. For this reason they are not addressed in the traditional literature. And precisely for this reason they must be addressed and articulated—for we do not find guidance with regard to these problems in traditional ethics and morality. Among these problems the protection of nature (and the protection of our life and of future generations) looms very large. Protection of nature, when seriously conceived, leads to a host of new strategies and indeed the idea of ecological ethics.

III

I have written on ecological ethics, and on eco-values, in my earlier publications (see especially *Dancing Shiva in the Ecological Age*, paperback edn., New Delhi, 1995). In this article I simply want to emphasize that the protection of nature cannot be a pious wishful-thinking activity, whereby we wish that other people should be less destructive of nature. Nor can it be merely a vigorous action of youg activists, who want to protect a given river bed or even the whole range of the Himalayas. It must be a *metanoia*, turning things inside out, establishing a new relationship with nature and with ourselves—but on a deep metaphysical level, and not through superficial exhortations: "let us save nature."

This new attitude to nature must be based on a new image of the world. We must view the *universe as a sanctuary*; not as a machine. In this sanctuary we need to behave as shepherds and as custodians. Some would even want to say as priests—reverentially and with deep respect to our sanctuary. Thus reverence for life and for our sanctuary/earth emerges as the basic ecological value. From this value immediately follows the second major value: responsibility *as reverence in action*.

The third major ecological value is *frugality, conceived as grace without waste*. Frugality, within our fragile planet, is so important that we need to elevate it to a moral virtue. Thus remember, you vote most importantly through your lifestyles—elegantly frugal or horrendously wasteful.

Now I am not saying that saving a river bed, and especially the Himalaya, through concerted actions is not important. But I am saying that this action must be accompanied by a new consciousness and new values (of reverence for life, of responsibility, of frugality). When we possess this new consciousness and are guided by new values, then we go into action with a new purpose and energy. Our action is then more rooted, more convincing and has better chances to succeed. Ultimately, we need to spread our new consciousness and our new values so that there is no necessity to fight for every threatened habitat—as we shall be guided by reverence and not greed.

The main battle for preserving the earth and for maintaining a meaningful future will be a moral one. This is one of the main points of my discourse.

IV

One of the practical extensions of eco-ethics is the idea of sustainable development, which is an umbrella concept containing a number of strategies, policy recommendations and also moral values. This idea was born in the 1980s when negative consequences of rampant technology, serving traditional development, became obvious. To be truly and genuinely sustainable, any development, in my opinion, should be:

— Ecologically responsible
— Economically vialble
— Socially equitable, and
— Culturally sensitive or culture-specific.

Any development which makes sense in the long run must be ecologically responsible. For if it leads to ecological ruin, what we witness is a process of ruination, not development.

Genuine development must be economically viable. It must be self-supporting in the long run. Yet this viability must be accountable not only in economic terms but simultaneously in social and ecological terms. If ecological consequences are neglected, we are back to the situation of the ecological ruination. Any development must be a rational enterprise. A form of development which leads to stupid ruinous consequences is not rational.

Meaningful and worthy development must be just and equitable. It must benefit not just the privileged individuals or societies which manipulate the whole process of development but local people, a vast majority of them. Sustainable development must fulfil the promise which material progress failed to deliver. It must be the vehicle of social and human amelioration. But it must not concentrate on one aspect of the human existence—the material well being. It must address itself to the entire human condition, including its psychological, social and spiritual aspects. Otherwise, it will become a failure, as material progress has already become. The possibility of this failure is lurking behind as too many people think of development, including sustainable development, in material terms alone.

Sustainable development should be culture—specific, sensitive to the conditions of the culture in which it takes place. Let us express this idea in stronger terms. *There isn't one universal model of development which is "best" for all environmental and cultural conditions.* Classical economics has laboured under the illusion that there is one universally valid economic knowledge—for all human cultures and circumstances. The truth is that each culture needs a model of development which is suitable to its history and its characteristics. Only such a model, which is very sensitive to the cultural milieu, can succeed as a truly sustainable model.

Seen from a larger perspective, sustainable development implies sustainable lifestyles and sustainable values, which we cherish and want to perpetuate. The three realms co-define and support each other, they are a trinity within the unity.

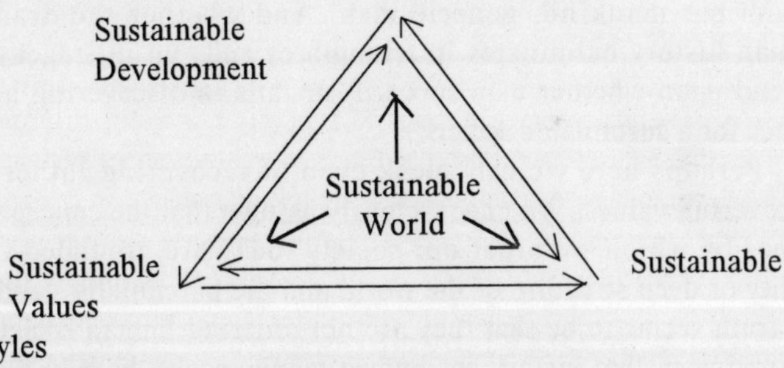

Each side of the triangle implies the other two. Sustainable development will not be possible if it is accompanied by wasteful lifestyles and purely materialist values of consumption. We live a unitary world to such a degree that it almost boggles our mind.

The ethics of solidarity, participation, empathy and compassion which the conception of the new sustainable world requires, only echoes ancient teachings, namely, that all people are one, all the world is one, and that we must live in peace in order to survive and in order to enter the High Road which ultimately leads to liberation, self-actualization and happiness.

8

HUMAN VALUES FOR A SUSTAINABLE SOCIETY

—LATE KRISHNA CHAITANYA

Whether we in India are heading towards or away from a sustainable society is a question which it has become impossible today to discuss in isolation from the comprehensive issue of the direction in which the whole world is moving because, for good or ill, the entire earth has become a single arena or stage. The hero—or anti-hero depending on the role chosen—is not any individual or nation but mankind, generic man. And whether the drama of human history culminates in triumph or ends up in tragedy will depend upon whether man succeeds or fails in discovering human values for a sustainable society.

Perhaps here we can speak even of recovering rather than discovering values. We unconsciously assume that the concepts and values by which we order our society today are grounded in the reality or deep structure of the world and are perennially valid. But the truth seems to be that they are not ordering human society but destroying it, that history has known many epochs, both in the east and the west, which were organised on different values and that they succeeded in sustaining society. The most important feature of these value-systems and world-views of older epochs is that they linked life on earth with a transcendental order, saw evolution as the working out of a blueprint from beyond space and time, read the drama of human history as the sequel of a prologue in heaven.

The most distinguishing feature of modern world-views is that they deny this vertical dimension to life on earth. But attempts have been made to derive principles of social ordering from this perspective which is confined to the foreground and has no depth. For instance, biologist George Gaylord Simpson has claimed: "Man was certainly not the goal of evolution, which evidently had no goal. He was not planned, in as operation wholly planless." Nevertheless he has argued that since man has somehow arrived on the scene, he can think morally and accept imperatives which will create a sustainable human society. Julian Huxley also thought along the same lines, about an "emergent religion of the future" which would dispense with the linkage of the human with the divine. He wrote: "It should be possible, with our increased knowledge of mind, to define man's sense of right and wrong more clearly so as to provide a better moral support, and to focus the feeling of sacredness on fitter objects." He felt certain that the world-view he shared with Simpson would enable "the fuller realisation of life's possibilities as a sacred trust." The ethical imperatives which Sartre accepted with deep conviction-authenticity or integrity, an almost Kantian insistence that man has to behave in such a manner that others will consider it worthy of emulation and the generalised behaviour pattern will sustain society-are identical with those of the older world-views. But, denying essence, Sartre cannot convincingly validate these imperatives for existence. They are shallow in depth, merely man-deep, not world-deep, and it is very clear from the predicament of modern man that these imperatives have been rejected; and the reason may be their ontological shallowness.

Theodore Roszak paid a fully merited tribute to Schumacher when he reviewed the latter's last book, *A Guide for the Perplexed.* But he also stressed the inadequacy of even the wisest advice meant to restore the lost meaning of life when it does not begin by squarely confronting the vast negation of our time. He added: "It is naive to summon us to self-knowledge without acknowledging that the deepest self-knowledge of our time begins in the experiencing of radical absurdity and cosmic abandonment. Self-knowledge for us must go through Nietzsche, Kafka, Sartre, Beckett, not around them." Roszak here points to two very important truths which are among the most valued among the old Indian perceptions too. If we are not to be engulfed by a sense of cosmic abandonment, we must have a true knowledge of our self, for it evolved in the world and its growth and well-being depend upon aligning with the laws of the world's working whose benignity it was that led evolution to the creation of man. In the Gita, in the passage where Krishna enumerates all the splendid creations of evolution and affirms them to be manifestations of the splendour of the creator, he makes the very significant statement that, of all sciences or disciplines of knowledge, he is the *science of the self.* He adds that man realises his fullest growth, or destroys *himself*, through his own action. He defined Yoga, the informed behaviour that will enrich man's being, as "*skill in action*". We have to be very careful in understanding the meaning of this. Today the management, really the mismanagement, of the world has been taken over by people who have the greatest skill in manipulative action, in misguiding men. But the skill in action Krishna meant has been clarified by traditional commentary as skill in discriminating action that is of moment to the spirit from action that is injurious to it. Knowledge used without wisdom changes great possibility into dark fatality, for it is such knowledge that generates action which destroys instead of sustaining.

This leads to the second important truth latent in Roszak's observation. The names of the thinkers he mentions are enough to evoke today's landscape of desolation, a world where God is dead (Nietzsche), living is encountering cruel and irrational riddles (Kafka), man's existential ontology has no link with essence (Sartre) and he waits in vain for someone who can redeem him (Beckett). But it is not enough if we content ourselves by analysing the grievous errors in the thought of these and similar thinkers. For, just as the modern psyche has been moulded by them, they were themselves moulded by the erroneous thinking of scientism which began further back and which we must distinguish from genuine science. In the reconstruction of this science, along with today's rather belated perceptions, we can recall old Indian insights too for, if forgotten, they still abide in our psyche and, recalled, are likely to have greater redemptive efficacy for us.

Modern thought began to drift in a fatefully, fatally, erroneous direction when science began to reduce the reality of the world and existence to the behaviour of matter and, further, misread that behaviour. Galileo studied the motions of bodies on the earth. Kepler studied the motions of vast aggregates of matter like the planets and Newton integrated their findings to formulate a universal law: the brick of the universe is the atom or particle of matter which is dead, inert, incapable of motion and moves only when pushed or pulled by an external force. On this physics was errected a biology of merely reflex action that made organisms mere marionettes or puppets which were helplessly reactive, jerking compulsorily to stimulus, and were not pro-active by themselves. This biology explained the appearance of many species of living organisms as due to random, wholly fortuitous genetic mutations that were weeded out by natural selection which latter was conceived as a bitter, murderous, survival struggle. Then science proceeded to create, on the basis of such physics and biology, a psychology of no psyche or an irrational and unconscious psyche which made all reasoning a crafty rationalisation by a turbulent, self-centred ego. From such presumptions it was easy for Adam Smith to derive a theory of economics which asserted that man could act only from self-interest and which, furtuer, blessed this self-interest by blandly affirming that a hidden providence, an *"invisible hand", could create the prosperity of all from the selfishness of each.* As Hofstadter has shown, this doctrine became the *philosophy of entrepreneurship* first in the west and then everywhere. The economics of self-interest captured politics and made it the horsetrading (in the so-called democracies) or murderous strife (in fascist polities) of pressure groups and power blocs.

Thus has been built up a *massive overburden of anti-human thought and values which may well suffocae mankind to extinction.* Everyone of these theories makes its contribution in destroying the synergy without which the family of mankind or of a nation or of even a village community cannot become a reality though it is the economic and political theories which are most widely perceived today as hostile to harmony. The Gita has a profound and precise analysis of the warping of human nature by anti-human thinking that creates different kinds of people who all tend to destroy synergy. The Gita's Tamasic man anticipates the mass man or the man of the mass society studied first by Ortega y Gasset and then by many thinkers. The mass-man abdicates responsibility and becomes totally pliable to the manipulations of the so-called leaders. In India we see the terrible consequence of this abdication when men with minds degenrate into mindless mobs who have rendered Indian society almost totally unsustainable in Ayodhya and elsewhere.

But the Gita also cites an equal threat from the Rajasic man, who corresponds to today's active exploiter of the world's resources, both natural and human, the man behind the big corporation, the multinational. After the lethargy of the era of political serfdom, there has been a tremendous release of energy in India. This would have been a good thing if the leaders in the forefront of this drive had kept before them the idea of building up a sustainable society in India which in fact was the ideal that sustained our independence struggle. But we have appallingly massive evidence that they did not do this: the enormous growth of secret funds built up in foreign banks by Indian entrepreneurs and of black money in circulation; the seizure by affluent sections of most of the funds provided for projects meant for the amelioration of people at and below the poverty line. This brings us back to the Gita's warning that the Rajasic man without a social conscience may become the Asuric man. This is the type of person who is convinced that the world is not established on a moral order (*apratishtham*), it is not built up on reciprocities (*aparaspara-sambhutam*), it is motored solely by the aggressive thrust of each individual's self-centred libido (*kamahaitukam*). The Gita also states that though such people will ultimately perish, they will do immense havoc to the world before they fall. Today in India corrupt practices in public life of immense magnitudes do get exposed, but after they have done colossal damage to society.

Old perceptions, integrated with the most modern, indicate that this antisocial and antihuman reading of the world by the Rajasic turned Asuric is erroneous all along the line, from the physics of the particle to the analysis of the psyche or self of man. The ancient Greeks too reduced the variety of matter to the primordial particle, but this particile was affirmed to be ensouled. The *Bhagavata* affirms that the physical particle is *chid-achidanmaya*, it has both material and metnal dimensions. And the particle in quantum physics has a power of self-movement or internal determinism conclusively established in a hundred experiments. According to the Samkhya theory of evolution, further refined by the Gita, it is a goal-oriented or teleological thrust in life that has created more and finer sense organs for the organism's understanding of the world and more and more efficient motor organs for its action on the world. And with Bertalanffy and others, modern evolution theory is returning to this conviction.

But the perception that can contribute most to the possibility of man creating a sustainable society is that of the world as a designed system. Today it is gaining strength in the growing current of thought stimulated by the Gaia Hypothesis of James

Lovelock. Gain is the earth conceived as the mother goddess of sustainable life in ancient Greek myth. Identical preceptions are there, with greater richness of detail and profundity of insight, in the great Hymn to Earth in the Atharva Veda. The Gita gives it a splendid substantiation and through a condensed but vivid and adequate summation of the world's process and its teleology. Krishna refers to the heat of the sun that vaporises the waters into clouds that bring the rain that causes to sprout the flora that sustains the fauna and mankind. Bracket any process in nature and you shall find that while its occurrence (its how) can be explained in terms of antecedent causes, its rationale (its why) can be explained only in terms of the purpose it serves and this purpose reaches far beyond the bracketing. And Krishna adds that the man who does not work in this manner, which is the way the vast world works and which sustains the totality, human society and its life support systems in nature, lives in vain; in fact he commits sin.

Sin or sacrilege is the violation of a great law or design of harmony which, in the light of its roots that go deep into the very structure of the world, has to be considered as a sacred design. Hans Jenas has said that there is no hope for man, for a sustainable society, if we do not recover the sense of the sacred which has been destroyed by the convergence of many lines of erroneous thinking over several centuries. Like the rest of the world, we in India too have lost all sense of the sacred, have become addicted to sacrilege. We make cosmetic, futile anti-pollution gestures while continuing to generate toxic effluents that pollute the air and our great rivers like the Ganga, once considered sacred. We indulge in a little social forestry while destroying our forests at a colossal rate. While Freud riveted the self of man to absolute determinism, the thrust of humanistic psychologists like Maslow, Rogers, May, Frankl and others has restored freedom to the self. But we should remember the Gita's warning that if man is free to work for an order of justice for all, he may also abuse his freedom and wreck the world and himself. For the purposes of parading and publicity, *we have any number of programmes for a sustainable society. They cannot redeem us when we have rejected the values that can sustain society.* Let us ever remember that the last verse of the Gita does not affirm that a sustainable society will be established but says only that it *can be* established if there is a partnership between man and God in the creation of history. Here 'God' need not necessarily mean a theistic belief; but it certainly means *world-conserving values*. Without recovering them, all our programmes of conservation, of nature and human society, will flounder. History is open-ended. It can steadily progress or get derailed and wrecked. Whatever happens will be our doing.

9

VALUES
The Invisible Power
(for Sustainable Development)

—PROF. R.K. MOHAPATRA

Background

The power of Money is known to one and all starting from a toffee buying Child to a luxury cruise buying Billionaire.

In the process of evolution of Human Society, due to the difficulty of organising the *tangible/physiological needs*, such as food, shelter, clothing, etc., the main orientation of the society has remained centred around *Economic Activities (System)* like Production, Consumption and Exchange of economic goods, giving Money its due importance as the measure of value of economic goods.

Therefore the focus has remained on *Economic Development* since the beginning of the *Process of Planned Development*, not only in India, but all over the world.

Accordingly the Development thinking at UN agencies till 1989 was influenced by the belief that *Economic Aspects of Development are Primary and the Social Aspects* will be automatically be taken care of by the fruits of Economic Development through *Trickle Down Effect*.

The realisation comes only when *Growing Economic Achievements* without equitable redistribution of income as well as neglect of social institutions, have *Generated Social unrest* as happened in the West in the seventies, who looked towards India for an answer.

Chairman, Vision Foundation of Development Management.

Ultimately the Trickle Down Theory failed, but why?

The Questions?

What is the cause(s) of the people accumulating economic wealth beyond their basic needs, which hinders equitable redistribution of economic resources and increase in the productivity of the economic system?

This question remains unanswered.

UN agencies particularly UNDP under the leadership of Mr. Mahbub ul Haq, principal author and coordinator of the HDI (Human Development Index) and special adviser to UNDP Administrator, have brought in revolutionary changes in the Development Thinking by focusing on the Social Sector.

But it seems (as per the extract of HDR, 1995 given below) that the answer to the question mentioned above has not been sought even when it is realised that Economic growth does not lead to Human Development.

The Human Development Report (Page 23)

The first Human Development Report (1990) developed the concept of human development and its measurement. It also explored the relationship between economic growth and human development. It showed that:

— The link between economic growth and human progress is not automatic. Fairly respectable levels of human development are possible even at fairly modest levels of income. And high GDP growth in several countries has failed to benefit their people.

— An external environmental favourable to growth is vital to support human development strategies in the 1990s.

Successive Reports focused on specific issues of human development in the larger perspective set forth in the first one. The 1991 Report tried to answer this basic question: is it possible to restructure the present expenditure pattern of developing countries and aid allocations to finance the basic human priorities in these countries?

The conclusion was that it is often the absence of political will, and not always the lack of financial resources, that is responsible for human neglect.

The 1992 Report examined the international perspective and the external environment for national human development efforts. It concluded that trade and financial opportunities in international markets are needed even more than aid to enhance human development initiatives in developing countries.

The basic theme of the 1993 Report was people's participation, it assessed how much people participated in the decisions and processes that shape their lives. It also made concrete suggestions for a new people-centred world order.

The 1994 Report introduced new concept of human security—the security of people in their homes, in their jobs, in their communities and in their environments. It identified the profound policy changes in national and global management required by this new concept of human security.

A critical shortfall of development in the past few decades has been the persistent neglect of the creativity and productivity of half of humanity. The same is true of human development debates and dialogues. In most cases, they have touched gender issues—but not really focused on them.

The four critical elements of the human development concept—productivity, equity, sustainability and empowerment—demand that gender issues be addressed as development issues and as human rights concerns. The compelling reason: development, if not engendered, is endangered. Only when the potential of all human beings is fully realized can we talk of true human development. The 1995 Report thus focuses on gender and development.

The issue-based Human Development Reports of UNDP fail to look at Sustainable Development with a holistic approach. To my mind, for *Sustainable Human Development*, it is essential to know the answer to the question above and understand Sustainable Development as a System.

The Answer

The answer to the above question is *Values*, where:

— Values are powerful determinants to human behaviour in

individuals, groups and society as a whole.

— Values provide a ready-made means for judging the social worth of persons and pluralities.
— Values focus the attention of people upon material, cultural items that are considered desirable, useful and essential.
— The ideal ways of thinking and behaving in any society are indicated by values. Blueprint of socially accepted behaviour so that people can almost discern the "best" way of acting and thinking.
— Values act as guideposts for people in their choice and fulfilment of social roles.
— Values act as a means of social control and social pressure.
— Values function as a means of solidarity.

We can take a parallel from the relationship of the body and mind in a human system to the relationship of an Economic System and Social System in a Human Development process and one can clearly make out how the conditions of Body and Mind are interdependent, just like the coditions of an Economy and the Society of a State.

Simply put, the Economic Behaviour like accumulating wealth more than basic needs, adoption of illegal means to accumulate wealth is controlled by the thinking/Social Values of an individual.

If we try to develop a model of *Sustainable Development*, we need to provide equal emphasis on the tangible and intangible needs of human beings and thereby the economic and social systems of a nation, which will essentially mean developing a model for social development as a parallel to the economic development.

Now, to understand the cause of Economic Growth not automatically resulting in Human Development or in other words, why does an individual withhold wealth after his basic needs are met, we need to understand the total Development Process as a system, in which Economic and Social sub-systems operate in an integrated manner.

If Sustainable Human Development is related to the Quality of Life, which in turn depends upon the degree to which Human Needs are satisfied, we can refer to Maslow's Need Hierarchy given below, which contains a set of Tangible needs like Food Shelter, Clothing, etc. at the bottom end of the hierarchy (closer to animal) and a set of Intangible needs like Self-esteem, Self-actualisation, Belongingness, love, etc.

Maslow's Need Hierarchy

5th : the Self-Actualization Needs: Self-development and Realization.
4th : the Esteem Needs: Self-esteem, Recognition and Status.
3rd : the Social Needs: Sense of belonging, love.
2nd : the Safety Needs: Security and Protection.
1st : the Physiological Needs of Hunger, Thirst, (Food, Shelter, Clothing).

Here the economic system provides for the tangible needs and the social system provides for the intangible needs.

We may note that after the Economic Success in the West the Western People were coming to India and are still coming to search for meaning of Life, the cause of peace amidst Poverty, the strength of Indian Society.

Because Human Development is centred around the Human Being and its Tangible (Economic Needs) and Intangible (Social Needs), there is an inter-relationship/dependence between the two.

Let us go through the case given below based on real life experiences. I am sure many of the readers might have come across similar experiences.

There are two companies in Delhi named M/S X and M/S Y, manufacturing and marketing Auto Parts. Both the companies are manufacturing same parts and distributing in the same territory, both employ about 100 employees.

Summarily, both the companies are in same or similar Economic Systems, but the difference lies in the Values of the 100 employees, influenced by the values of the Chief Executive/Owner.

When in M/S X, the Values are positive reflected by punctuality, sincerity, negligible absentism, no/marginal pilferage, it is negative in M/S Y reflected by absentism, late coming, pilferage, etc.

The result of this difference in value system is reflected in terms of Low cost of production low brakage, wastage, rejection, higher profits, more income (bonus, etc.), more employment leading to promotion of positive social values and in case of M/S Y, it is high cost of production, low profits or loss, low income, loss of employment leading to frustration, social crimes like drugs, theft, etc. leading to promotion of negative social values.

From the above case the *Power of Values* can be clearly appreciated in terms of its ability to:

(a) contribute to economic success in the long run, and
(b) strengthen the Social Value System.

Thus *Values* are primary in the Human Development System, as Life-Force/Spirit to Human Living Until and unless we realise the essence of the *Values*, sustainable Human Development will remain a dream.

In a Society charged with negative values, individuals earn more wealth through illegal means, more than needed to meet their basic needs, will have more Greed to retain wealth, which will cause concentration of economic power and hinder redistribution of wealth and also cause poverty and sufferings for a section of the society causing social tensions.

Any short-term economic growth process cannot be sustained in absense of Positive Values as it happened in the Eighties in the world, when American economy following a value system represented by Individualism, power for the self, etc. was overtaken by Japan following a Value System represented by family values.

We need to compare the two primary sub-systems of Sustainable Human Development in more detail through the table given below:

Parallels between Economic and Social Development Systems

1. *Parameters*	*Economic System*	*Social System*
Activities	Production, Consumption, Exchange of goods	Production (performing social norms/ behaviour/values), Consumption (being benefit to others, when one follows

		positive social norms/behaviour/ values)
2. Medium of Transactions	Money	Values
3. Money is generated by	Undertaking economic activities, like production, sale, purchase, consumption, etc. which satisfies the tangible needs of the population	
Values are developed by:	Conducing social transactions in a manner that reinforces Values and satisfies the intangible needs of the population, thereby creating social examples for imitation	
5. Measure of strength:	Balance of payment, Power of Currency	Recognition of values of a nation in the global level
6. Source of strength:	Natural Resouces, Climatic Conditions, etc.	History, Cultural Heritage, Great Epics, Contribution of religious leaders
7. Symptoms of crisis:	Unemployment, starvation, Negative BOP, Failure to meet Debt obligation	Social Degradation, social injustice reflected by abnormal social behaviour and social crimes, like father raping daughter, in-laws killing the daughter-in-law, Family disorder

Thus we can conclude that Social Values have the power to increase the productivity of Economic System and ensure equitable redistribution of the fruits of economic growth to the whole society and therefore Values can be termed as *source of invisible power for Sustainable Human Development.*

So we have a duty to promote positive values for sustaining the process of Development.

PART II

STUDIES OF INSTITUTIONS ENGAGED IN VALUE SYSTEMS

10

A BRIEF REPORT ON IMPORTANT FEATURES OF VALUE-BASED EDUCATION IN SRI SATHYA SAI INSTITUTE OF HIGHER LEARNING PRASANTHI NILAYAM

—PROF. MULK RAJ CHILANA* AND P.H. SETHUMADHAVA RAO**

In pursuance of the communication received from the Ministry of Human Resource Development, a Committee consisting of Dr. Mulk Raj Chilana, Professor of Education, NCERT and Dr. P.H. Sethumadhava Rao, Joint Secretary, UGC, visited Sri Sathya Sai Institute of Higher Learning Prasanthi Nilayam from 29th February to 5th March, 1992 to study value-based education imparted at the Institute.

2. The Members of the Committee were expected to understand the organisation of the institution and to interact with the trustees of Sathya Sai Education Society with a view to study the feasibility of incorporating some of the important features of value-based education being imparted in the institution under the society. It was naturally expected that the team would understand the content of value education programme and find out how the working of the institution leads to better learning of values by students. The Committee was also expected to study as to what could be done to extend the influence and halo of the institution far and wide in India.

3. The mode of work of the Committee included scanning through the available literature, attending the classrooms, meeting with the staff and students, visit to Planetarium and Eternal

* Consultant School of Practical Philosophy, Johannesberg, South Africa.

** Joint Secretary, University Grant Commission, New Delhi.

Heritage Museum and observation of the atmosphere on the campus. The Committee had the privilege of blessings and advice from Bhagwan Sri Sathya Sai Baba and noticed the serenity of atmosphere during the period Bhagwan gave *darshans* in the mornings and evenings. The members of the Committee met several times Professor S. Sampath, Vice-Chancellor, Sri K. Chakravarthi, Registrar and Professor H. Najundaiah, Controller of Examinations. There were meetings with a number of other prominent faculty members of different departments, schools and other important centers. Some of the names are given.

4. The Committee also visited Sri Sathya Sai Higher Secondary School and its Primary Wing and held discussions with the Principal and Vice-Principal of the school. One of the Committee Members attended the morning assembly of the school on Thursday, the 5th March, 1992. The Committee also went around the school campus, college campus and saw the residential arrangements made for the students. Thus they got the firsthand experience of how human values are practised in the institute.

5. Sri Sathya Sai Institute of Higher Learning Prasanthi Nilayam was recognised as a Deemed University by the erstwhile Ministry of Education of the Government of India and the U.G.C. in the year 1981. Revered Bhagwan Sri Sathya Sai Baba is the Chancellor of the Deemed University for his lifetime. The institute has three separate campuses at present, its two campuses for men are at Prasanthi Nilayam and at Brindavan and the third campus for women is located at Anantpur. The Institute can, with the prior approval of the Government of India, establish campuses in any part of the country.

6. The Institute believes in promoting national integration in the best possible way. As such it follows the policy of open admission and attracts students to join their studies from all parts of the country. The admission is made purely on the basis of merit irrespective of income, class, creed and religion.

7. Sri Sathya Sai Institute of Higher Learning accords very high priority to the programme of value education. The students have unique opportunity to live in a wholesome community life and pursue the academic excellence, knowledge and wisdom combined with values like duty and devotion. They also learn meditation, yoga, games and service to the community alongwith other seekers of truth.

8. Many special features of the Institute contribute to make the campus atmosphere conducive for intellectual growth and value development among the students. The Institute is unique indeed for having excellent laboratories. The centre for computer science is comparable with the best of such centres in other parts of the country. The Institute has a modern planatorium which helps in increasing understanding of the basic concepts of astronomy, mathematics, science and other related disciples. The spiritual museum on the campus imparts knowledge of human values inherited from the Vedic times. The Institute has highly dedicated, competent and motivated teachers drawn from different parts of the country. That makes the institution most unique is its focus, in addition to academic excellence, on the development of correct attitudes and values among the students in order to shape them as leaders in scientific, civic and professional enterprises.

9. The Committee members discovered that the programmes of value education in the Institute are not sporadic; but they stem from the fundamental Sai Philosophy of Education which is known as 'Integral Education'. The major goal of the system is transformation of both the individual and the society. Truly emerging from the general philosophy of life, the theory of integral education stands for full blessing of human excellence so as to nurture human personality in all aspects—physical, mental, emotional, psychic, and spiritual. This experiment in integral education places human values at the forefront. The envisioned goal of Sri Sathya Sai system of education is all-round development of individual so that he may be able to play a dynamic role in service of the society.

10. The Institute provides a very befitting answer to an important question as to what should constitute the 'Content' of value education for our secular society with diverse background of many religions and cultures. Based on research and long experimentation, Sathya Sai organisation has evolved a framework of five basic values of 'Truth, Righteous Conduct, Peace, Love and Non-Violence'. Named as 'Education for Human Values', the programme aims at harmonious development of an individual at cognitive, affective and conative levels. The assimilation of these values assures best possible nurturing of a human personality resulting in the resolution of inner and outer conflicts. This full vision of human potential and social needs provides prodigious

foundation for further work in other parts of the country.

11. While the programme broadly encompasses the above-stated basic values, sincerity for the cause in the Institute is evident from the course content which lists 'sub-values' under each of the five major values. The sub-values are also truly secular and universal in character. For instance, sub-values for developing 'Love' include caring, compassion, generosity, sharing, patience, tolerance, kindness, forgiveness and many others. Under 'Peace' some values are, humility, self-discipline, patience, contentment and endurance. Similarly, sub-values of honesty, integrity, self-knowledge, self-analysis and synthesis under 'Truth'; of duty, ethics, gratitude, sacrifice and simplicity under 'Right Conduct' and concern for life, brotherhood, social justice and service to others are identified under 'Non-Violence'. These are only examples of the sub-values which have been developed after intensive work of more than a decade. Discussion with teachers revealed that any list of values could in no way be claimed as exhaustive. Teachers are supposed to develop their own values as per needs of the students and the circumstances in which instructions are conducted.

12. Another very significant aspect of the programme is 'How' of value education. This includes both the curricular revision and the co-curricular aspects of the instructional programme. In an ideal condition value education should constitute an integral part of the educational curriculum. However, the common core components may be emphasised in some separate sessions also. The Committee was informed that teachers in the Institute follow all the three methods of direct instruction, indirect teaching and mixed techniques of both while dealing with the nature of values to be imbibed by the students. The maximum impact was of the personal example of the teachers. The methods followed by the teachers for value education are reported to be stories, role plays, dramas, skits, silent sitting, national and devotional aspects and other such activities. The students also hold discussions on the lives of eminent personalities like prophets and scientists as well as social workers. *Sarvadharam* prayer is conducted in the Institute with great sanctity. As far as the college students are concerned, the faculty members informed that lectures, round table conferences, formal and informal seminars and extension lectures are organised.

13. The Institute recognises that the teacher is the linchpin of

the value education programme. In addition to his knowledge and understanding, his feelings, actions and personal life influence the students a great deal. Thus, teacher is recognised as the most important in the programme. In the Sai Philosophy of Education, a teacher has been described as creator, preserver and destroyer of virtues of wisdom and of faith in the hearts of the children. High priority is, therefore, given to the training of teachers at pre-service level in value education. The syllabus for B.Ed. includes a full paper on value-based education. The paper is devoted to understanding the meaning, scope and organisation of values.

It also includes meaning and scope of five basic human values and methods and techniques of teaching human values. Tools for evaluation in human values include oral, written and observation forms. Students are expected to understand evaluation of cognitive, affective and conative levels. Besides the full paper, general foundation courses are prescribed in both the semesters. These courses provide the background of Indian culture, Indian Constitution, World Perspective and relationship of spirituality and science. Another elective paper is on moral and spiritual education. Major themes in the paper are yoga, the system of Indian philosophy, the sacred texts of Hindus, unity of religion and spiritual leaders of the world.

14. In order to facilitate the work of teachers for imparting value education, Sri Sathya Sai Society has prepared manuals for teachers. The publications include introduction to the basic values, methodology for teaching-learning interactions and evaluation of the outcomes. They include illustrations, quotations, poems and drawings. Similarly, lesson plans have been developed at different places of experimentation by the Society.

15. Daily routine of the students is one of the striking aspects of the work of the Institute. Since the Institute is residential, the students get up early in the morning. In fact, their day starts at 5.00 AM commencing with 'Suprabhat'. The students are taught *yoga asanas*. They have breakfast in the dining hall at 8.00 AM. in the morning. The activities of the schools and colleges commence with a prayer followed by a talk given by a student for about 10 minutes. There is a lunch break from 11.30 AM to 12.15 PM. The afternoon classes start at 2.15 PM. There are games during the day. In the evening, students assemble in the 'Mandir' to have the blessings of

Sri Sai Baba. The students take their seats silently and are seen engaged in their studies even while they are in the premises of the Mandir. Thus, they do not waste their time in any way. After the dinner, they go to bed by 9.00 PM. Students are allowed to meet their parents/guardians only on Sundays. They can go out with their parents only after seeking permission from their respective wardens. Every day there is a 'Thought for a Day' which proves as a source of inspiration. The Institute has many other good practices like silent sitting, community prayer and occasional addresses by eminent persons. Special programmes of longer duration are held on Thursdays including quizzes, debates, dramatic presentations and symposia etc.

16. Another silent feature of the Institute is semester system of studies with continuous and comprehensive internal evaluation. Laudable work has been done in the Institue for development of question banks. Adoption grading system ensures higher degree of objectivity in the evaluation of performance of the students. The Institute has always held examination reforms as an integral part of education initiative and integral part of educational initiative and innovations. As important point in this regard is that students are tested not only in their academic achievements but they are also tested in integral items such as *yoga asanas*, games and sports, attendance at universal prayer, meditation, readings on unity of religions, attendance in classes and contribution in self-reliance programmes. Statement of grades clearly indicates the grade secured in these items as well as in the academic areas. This enables the employers to select appropriate candidates for their jobs.

17. Another very significant yearly feature of the Institute of Higher Learning is organisation of a summer course attended by the faculty members and the students, including those newly admitted, of all the three campuses. The course is held in Brindavan campus and it is addressed by prominent experts, guest speakers and selected teachers. It may be worthwhile to have an intensive study of the summer course during the period when it is organised. This study will have a great potential for drawing lessons for organisation of similar courses at other places.

18. A course on awareness programme is also an important feature of the education system of Sri Sathya Sai Institute of Higher Learning. This course is spread over two years. It is an excellent

exposure to Indian culture as well as an opportunity for bringing better understanding of cultural heritage of mankind. The first semester is devoted to the Indian spiritual experiences. The second semester intends to acquaint the students with the cultural heritage of mankind. The third semester is devoted to the themes related with literature of the world. The fourth semester reviews the fundamental concepts in physical sciences and life sciences. An intensive study of this programme will provide many ideas for developing a suggested programmes for college students as well as for students of higher secondary classes.

19. Important events of the Institute are another source from where a lot of implications can be drawn for spreading the message to other institutions. Through these programmes, the Institute provides to the students experiences of the ideals of higher values which are essential in life. An impressive feature in this regard is annual festival of sports, games and cultural activities organised in the second week of January every year. In this programme, students of all the three campuses assemble at Prasanthi Nilayam to participate in various activities and to exhibit their talents. This is another important occasion when the reversed Chancellor presides over the function and blesses the students and the staff. Bakrid, Muharram and Milad-un-Nabi are the Muslim festivals celebrated on the campus. Christmas is celebrated with great zeal and fervour. Maha Shivratri, Ram Navami, Shri Krishna Janamashtmi are also celebrated. The major national events are celebration of Independence Day and Republic Day. The attempt, therefore, is to turn the holidays into holy days.

20. The work of Sri Sathya Sai Society in value education extends beyond the portals of schools and colleges. Their educational programmes extend value education activities to the special needs of the youth, women, parents and other such groups. The Sai educational Philosophy lays special stress on the role of the youth in improvement of the society as also to help them make the fullest use of their precious years. Social service by the Youth in villages is considered a significant spiritual exercise. Similarly vital role is expected to be played by the women. In order to recognize the prominence given to women, a special campus has been established so that girls may develop desirable qualities for meeting their sacred task of establishing better homes. Similarly, unique role of parents

has been visualised, especially for their help to their children to grow in amity and brotherly understanding of one another. Deeper studies may be made of the programme of value education for such sectors which fall under the arena of non-formal education.

21. Keeping in view the magnitude of the task of value education undertaken by Sri Sathya Sai Institute, there are many implications for extending the influence of these programmes to schools of all categories in the country. The programme of value education of the Institute at primary level is really pioneering because of the intensive nature of the activities undertaken such as types of values and sub-values, methodology of teaching and learning, evaluation, teachers' hand-books and lesson plans etc. Detailed write-ups of these may be made and disseminated far and wide in the country. Navodaya Vidyalayas may perhaps be the best beneficiaries to learn from these programmes. National level institutions like the NCERT may also have controlled experiments to try out some of their programmes as educational innovations in the area of value education. Similarly, programme of value education in secondary and senior secondary sections of the Institute may be studied. It will be of special significance for the schools to study the programme of daily routine of the students as well as the impact of the celebration of important yearly events in the Institute. Many lessons can be drawn from the awareness programme as well as summer course for different types of schools in the country.

22. There are also many implications of the findings for the education system at the college and post-graduate levels. The University Grant Commission has taken two important steps for implementing value education: (i) requesting universities to introduce a foundation course; and (ii) to request the universities to have a minimum of 180 work days. However, the Committee observed that Sri Sathya Sai Institute has more than 200 working days and the examinations are conducted regularly on the dates announced by the Institute. The results are also declared on the scheduled dates. If a holiday has to be observed in the Institute for any reason, this is made up by making sunday as a working day. The Institute continues to work with the semester and grading system, though some of the universities have reverted book to the old system. Other unique features of the Institute such as imparting an awareness programme in the form of foundation course, the

examination reforms, integration of science and spirituality can be followed by other colleges and universities with suitable adaptations to their own conditions.

23. While searching for the main features of value based education in the Institute, the members of the Committee felt that many prominent aspects of the programme require case studies through close observation and interviews with the students, teachers and even the parents. The five-fold system of values of Sri Sathya Sai Institute is undoubtedly self-consistent and based on workable theory of development of human personality. It is, therefore, recommended that controlled experimentation of the value education programme of this Institute may be undertaken in other institutions of the country. The schools and colleges elsewhere may completely adopt the system or introduce the same with suitable adaptations. But the message of the pace-setting story of Sri SAthya Sai Institute of Higher Learning and Sri Sathya Sai Society must be disseminated not only to schools, colleges and universities but also to parents and the community at large, using a wide spectrum of communication media. This would require more intensive studies of the whole system of value-based education as well as individual studies of its distinguished ingredients like curriculum, methodology, teacher training, awareness programme, summer institute, physical education, athletics, drama, adventure activities, debates and other co-curricular activities. Further studies may also be developed about the philosophy of education of Bhagwan Sri Sathya Sai Baba, as it emanates from his philosophy of life and crystallizes into the value system to be provided through education.

24. The members of the Committee are quite aware of the constraints which affect the quality of their observations. The report of the committee is far from any claim to be definitive because of the short time of only two full working days available to them for visits to schools and colleges and for observation of multifarious activities of the Institute. It could also not be possible for the members of the Committee to interact with the trustees of Sri Sathya Sai Education Society because of their not being available in Prasanthi Nilayam. Again, members of the Committee could not visit the other two campuses of the Institute at Brindavan and Anantpur. It has also not been possible to study the performance of the alumini of the Institute and their impact on the society at large.

25. The courtesy and kindness shown and the assistance received from one and all connected with the university is gratefuly acknowledged. Help from Professor S. Sampth, Vice-Chancellor and Sh. K. Chakravarthi, Registrar was extremely valuable and it facilitated substantially interaction with the knowledgeable colleagues in schools, colleges and administration. The Members of the Committee are conscious of their inability to repay the debt of gratitude to revered Chancellor Bhagwan Sri Sathya Sai Baba for His blessings and guidance.

11

VALUE EDUCATION IN DAYALBAGH EDUCATIONAL INSTITUTE

Work Culture with Values

—MULK RAJ CHILANA

Basic Foundation

Dayalbagh Educational Institute is now a Deemed University. It was started as a Middle School in 1917 by Shri Sahib Ji Maharaj, the Fifth Guru of Radhaswami faith. The school was raised to the level of High School within six months. It became an Intermediate College in 1922 and a Degree College in 1947. In the Year 1981, the Institute was noticed as a Deemed University. The Institute is a good example of dedicated and sincere efforts in building up an integrated educational complex consisting of Faculty of Art. Faculty of Commerce and Management, Faculty of Education, Faculty of Engineering, and Faculty of Science.

The Institute has a unique distinction of combining academic excellence with human values and principles related with our modern times. The Institute is a fine example of dedicated and sincere effort in building up an integrated educational complex. Their programmes of work experience, service to the community and combining education with values of all teachings related with 'Sant Mat' are well known to the people in India and abroad.

Distinctive Programmes

Besides different faculties, as stated above, various components of the programmes at undergraduate level include academic study of two major subjects and two courses to be selected from interdisciplinary and ancillary electives. Work-based training includes a work experience course related to one of the major subjects opted, by the students. This enables students to work with their own hands and to develop skills as well as generate a spirit of self-reliance. The core courses studied compulsorily by all undergraduate students include Indian culture, comparative study of religions, scientific methodology and rural development. The pursuit of co-curricular activities aims at building of an all-round personality of students through cultural and literary activities, games and sports, and social service. The other programmes in the Institute are PG Diploma in Computer Science and Application and PG Diploma in Textile Designing and Printing. A significant feature in all these programmes is inculcation of values among students so that they can become complete men and bring about physical, intellectual, emotional and ethical integration. They are supposed to develop the basic values—humanism, secularism and democracy.

Major Objectives

The objectives of the Dayalbagh Educational Institute (DEI) are development of the complete man irrespective of caste, creed, race, religion, economic position or social status. Specific objectives of the DEI in terms of value education are imparting of education of excellence with ethical values for contemporary relevance. This includes nurturing of scientific temper, and training a person to live in technology-oriented society. It is also an important objective to provide human touch among the students so that they can mellow down the harshness of the mechanical work. This is done through the study of Humanities and Social Sciences. Promotion of cultural heritage of the country is an important objective of the Institute so that students may develop pride for the national ethos and may be saved from losing their moornings. A special attempt is made in the Institute to cultivate an understanding of various beliefs so that students may develop an attitude of tolerance. National Integration is one of the important goals of instructions in the Institute. 'Ahimsa' is another objective and teachers are encouraged to promote principles of temperance and non-violence. Last, though not the least, the Institute aims at getting the students interested in understanding the problems of rural areas so that they can contribute to the village economy and help the people in the backward areas.

Value Content

The Institute does not make any direct attempt to teach the echical and moral values to the students. The spirit of these values is ingrained in all activities of the students under the guidance of their teachers. Thus, the values are more lived than talked about. In many cases, students discover ethical values and social goals with the help of their teachers. The core courses provide the major place for promoting value education. They include cultural education, comparative study of religions, understanding of scientific methodology, general knowledge, current affairs and rural development. These courses bring about general awareness about the Indian Culture. The students are also acquainted with basic tenets of major religions and underlying fundamental unity among them. In understanding these aspects, scientific methods are made use of. Another important feature in the content is work experience programme. This programme is related to major subjects and it is focused on developing skills both for self-employment as well as for better employability. In this area, knowledge is also related to practical life. In order to understand rural development, theoretical study as well as practical work is undertaken by the students through cultural operations, national adult educational programme, national service scheme, extension activities and research programmes. The students attempt to take technology to the villages through regular activities as well as through special camps. Another way to learn values is by participation of students in cultural activities like debates, essay writing, story writing, poetry recitation, celebration of national days and organisation of music, sports and games.

Methods Followed

The methods of learning value education are varied and both direct as well as indirect. The major emphasis is on work culture of students who lead an austere, disciplined, dedicated and productive life. They live in a very harmonious atmosphere. Cooperative community life is a significant feature. Since the Institute provides opportunities for mixing up of students of different ages, as well as different disciplines, there are opportunities of living like in a family. The infrastructure of agriculture, industry, education, technical institutions, art and culture and such types of other subjects provides an excellent opportunity for interlinking of resqurces which ultimately lead to development of complete personality in the individuals.

It is really heartening to find that there are no student unions or staff associations which lead to strikes and halting of work. Of course, there are representatives of staff as well as students on the Academic Council, the Governing Bodies and various other committees. Though there have been seldom any strikes by the students, they are free to put up their grievances. They are very cooperative in extending all help to the Institute authorities. It may be mentioned in this regard that this type of discipline flows down from the excellent examples set by the people at the top. In this connection it may be relevant to mention that the key posts of Director, Registrar and Treasurer are honorary. So, only those persons are appointed who do not get any remuneration and are committed to the objectives of the Institute. Non-denominational prayers are also an important source of learning values. The other learning processes include group discussions, seminars, home and library assignments, practical work in the field and extension lectures by experts.

Evaluation Procedures

It is realised by the Institute that intangible human qualities like values are difficult to be assessed, but there are attempts to follow integrated evaluation procedures. This type of evaluation is more formative than its being summative alone. All the components of learning are evaluated. The evaluation is continuous with varied modes of testing, spread over in every semster. It may be pointed out that there are two semsters in a year. It may also be mentioned that the students attend for more than 200 working days in a year with an average of six hours' daily schedule. It may be pertinent to mention that overall evaluation of the university is very high in the eyes of society in general and employers in particular. It has been reported several times that students are selected only because of the personal qualities which they have imbibed during their students days. Their qualities of being sincere workers and committed professionals endear the employers and so they are preferred for selection for jobs.

General Observations

The Dayalbagh Educational Institute has earned a unique name for its contribution to produce men with academic excellence and who have sound base in human values. The Institute, however, experiences some difficulties in keeping its position as it is. The major difficulty in this regard is the selection of right types of teachers. This difficulty is especially felt for selecting teachers with non-traditional subjects like comparative study of religions. The difficulties are also created by other sister universities who refuse to provide equivalence to the degree of this Deemed University. The University authorities also find that their programmes of studies appear more tough to those students who come from traditional schools and colleges and enrol for further studies. This difficulty is further increased because the students in DEI come not only from local areas but also from other parts of the country. The University authorities also feel constraints with regard to getting sufficient funds from the UGC both for Plan and Non-Plan grants. This is reported to be the common difficulty of most of the Deemed Universities. In spite of these difficulties, the work of the University has been highly appreciated. It has been generally accepted that the tranquil atmosphere of the Institute keeps the people not only free from tension, but it also paves the way for innovative work and blossoming of creative ideas. The discipline and work ethos of the Institute are really striking. It is a unique educational institution as it integrates instructions with real life. The task of the institution appears to be exalting of human spirit.

12

BRAHMA KUMARIS ISHWARIYA VISHWA VIDYALAYA

Divine Values for the Golden Age

—MULK RAJ CHILANA

Fundamental Base

Brahma Kumaris World Spiritual University was founded in the year 1937 by revered Brahma Baba who had a series of visions of the better world. He envisaged a cogent and coherent world order which will emerge from the deteriorating moral standards of today.

The institution is not a university in modern academic sense because there is neither a fixed campus nor there is a formally appointed faculty. The concept of University for this institution is that everyone in future will come to embrace the spiritual base and help in the golden period to come. It is also visualised that the key message of the University will reach everyone. The Institution follows the belief that the law of action is inviolable. It signifies that we reap according to what we sow. Thus no one can escape the result of his or her Karma. One will suffer in this or the next life if one has caused suffering to others by violation of norms of good or moral action. So every one of us must act with a sense of responsibility. They consider that ignorance of the law of Karma is no excuse. Therefore, all men and women must acquire knowledge of what is good and what is bad action. It means moral education and ethical values are recommended not only for society, but they are also essential for the redemption of an individual. The inviolability of the law of Karma presupposes that reincarnation is an accepted fact. It also believes that the present day sufferings are mainly the result of ignorance of our identity. Having identified with the body, man's basic characteristics of love turn into sex -lust, attachment and greed. The rest of the negativities such as hatred and jealousy are the offshoots of these evils. So the institution evinces a firm belief that one must get the Knowledge of the real i.e., transcendental identity of a soul. This realisation will raise the level of awareness above others' limitations. The knowledge of one's spiritual identity widens one's horizon of thinking and liberates one from narrow tendencies. Thus the philosophical foundation of Brahma Kumaris Ishwariya Vishwa Vidyalaya is value orientation and moral education. Its spiritual precepts transcend narrow considerations and pave the way for effective ethical growth of an individual.

Varied Experiences

The Brahma Kumaris World Spiritual University (BKWSU) does not have any school, college or postgraduate department in any subject where formal instruction is imparted to students. However, the institution has experiences of organising a variety of activities related with moral education and value orientation. BKWSU has more than 2000 centres for their spiritual instructions. For these centres value education is an important ingredient of the curriculum. They hold creative workshops to instil the spirit of co-operation and vision of the better world. In these workshops teachers of schools and colleges as well as heads of institutions also participate and implement programmes in their respective institutional situations. The faculty members of these workshops also visit various departments of different universities in India and abroad. Some of them are appointed on the advisory boards of some schools. The BKWSU has a large number of school teachers, lecturers and professors who meet from time to time to discuss issues of moral education. The institution also organises seminars, workshops and conferences of educationists. The conferences are separately organised for the role of youth in improvement of society. The institution also conducts courses for personality development of younger children. Children from different educational centres visit them for consciousness training either with their parents or separately in groups. Some centres of the university have provision for boarding and lodging of a number of students. This provides them an opportunity to get trained in moral education as they have longer period of stay. The BKWSU holds every year a programme in

Mount Abu where students participate in cultural and social activities, besides the provision for lectures on varied themes and declamation contests etc. The institution has a special provision for training of in-service teachers in moral education on behalf of the Directorate of Education, Karnataka. Thus the past experience of BKWSU is very wide. Apart from imparting moral and spiritual education to children and youth, people in various fields are also covered. Such programmes are held for doctors, scientists, engineers, jurists, businessmen, industrialists, media persons, administrators, beaurocrats, social workers and politicians.

Value Content

The BKWSU believes in holistic education which helps in blossoming of the full human potential. Their stress is on not only providing academic experience but also on development of other aspects of human personality. They also stress on imparting education which leads to global thinking, emotional balance and above all, stability and right type of conduct in various spheres of life. Most important role of education is to build correct outlook and attitude in man and to transform his behaviour qualitatively as well. Education should lead to not only imparting information but it should work as a process of transformation that leads a person and his society to the goal of purity, peace and perfection.

In order to meet the objective of education, as mentioned above, the content of value education has been divided into three major parts viz. human values, moral values and spiritual values. Human values include world brotherhood, love, purity, goodwill, service, peace, sense of responsibility and duty and awareness of the wonderful gifts which are given by family, society, nature and culture and for which it is necessary to have a sense of gratitude to them. In moral values the eight aspects covered include truthfulness, honesty, integrity, fairplay, justice, fearlessness, civility and politeness, non-stealing and spirit of sharing. In the spiritual values, emphasis is laid on brahmacharya, tapas, non-violence in thought, word and deed, introvertedness, humility, spirit of sacrifice for the well being of others, contentment, surrender and feeling of gratitude towards the God and emotional stability. An attempt has been made to divide all these values into sub-values as also to see the inter-relatedness of different values like freedom from bias, jealousy, hatred and feeling of vengance, freedom from crookedness, freedom from arrogance and other major evils like lust, greed, anger and attachment. Similarly, under the major value of 'Love' one must develop qualities of seeing good quality in others, understanding, co-operation, being kind and sympathetic, forgiving and forgetting others, benevolence, kindness and compassion.

Learning Methods

The BKWSU adopts both formal and informal, direct and indirect and as well as self-teacher dominated learning methods. It advocates high place for value education in the curriculum. It also desires that value education should be imparted through co-curricular activities. The most important source for learning values is considered the teacher. Great significance is attached to the personality of the teacher. He has the major responsibility for providing congenial environment for value education. The personality of teacher has an effect on formal lessons in moral and value education.

The BKWSU has many dedicated persons serving in the field of education. Many retired teachers join their teaching force. It has also a large number of dedicated ladies who inspire students by their exemplary conduct and character. It must be mentioned that the BKWSU lays much emphasis on women doing this work. The founding father of the institution was of the firm opinion that women give a touch of tenderness and love and evoke upsurge of the divine potential more easily in the students. The major techniques and methods for developing value education are preparation of case histories for guidance of students, moral interpretation of events in history, analysis of biographical accounts of events of certain persons, life histories of persons of great moral heights and recitation of poems which can have impact to promote value education. The institution also uses other methods like dramas, role plays, silent meditation, group discussions, creative workshops, seminars, lectures, personal counselling. Stories and devotional songs are also appropriately used. Other related activities include celebration of festivals, eloqution contests and personal discussions. Another very significant event of the institution is organisation of a summer course every year which provides opportunities for community living and awareness about the needs of people around.

It must be mentioned that the institution strongly advocates that nobody should use alcoholic drinks or be addicted to drugs and smoking.

Related Literature

The institution has developed detailed syllabus as well as published many general books for promoting the cause of value education. The detailed syllabus has been developed for all classes of primary and secondary schools. To illustrate, syllabus in Classes I & II includes major topics like cleanliness, truth, love with fellow children, love for world animals and plants and general principles of good living. Good conduct and appropriate etiquette is given primary importance. For Classes III & IV more topics are added like development of qualities like patience, service, fearlessness, tolerance, honesty and simplicity. In higher classes spiritual experiences are also included. Similarly, environment, characteristics of Indian culture, national integration, renunciation and desire to discharge the responsibilities are also incorporated. Some lessons have also been developed to inculcate desired good qualities among students.

The institution has also prepared literature which enlightens the students on the significance of moral and human values in life. It also publishes three magazines which provide materials for teachers so that they themselves can make rapid progress for developing of values among students. This facilities the teachers for undertaking the work of value education. The books on moral and human values aid in self-transformation among various levels of people. The BKWSU has also formulated certain codes of ethics for various professions. The books have very attractive titles. There are 'moral values', 'attitudes and moods', 'yuva jago', 'youth charter', 'Divya Guno ka Guldusta', Vikari per Vijay', 'just a moment', and 'Kamalpushp Sum Jivan'.

Apart from the literature mentioned above, there are cassettes of lectures on moral themes. There are also some sets of pictures which are used during exhibitions. Another source of value education is a collection of slogans which are used as 'Subhashitam' or 'Nitivachan'.

Evaluation Tools

The major tool of evaluation in the BKWSU is the observation of the conduct and behaviour of the students during all activities. The students are observed while playing, while at work and even when they are living in the community as also during their studies. Besides the reporting by teachers, parents are also involved in evaluating the impact of value education. In addition, comments of fellow students are given due importance. The means of evaluation are both oral and written tests. Again, the aspects to be evaluated include cognitive, affective and conative domains. Practical experiences interms of action are also given due importance.

A very important feature of the evaluation scheme of the institution is the significance given to self evaluation. They stress that one should know one's place in the scheme of things and one's role in the drama of life. One must also realise one's potential for good and how one can honestly fulfil one's deeper and finer aspirations. If one rises to this level, only then one can reject what is unworthy and accept what is worthy. The BKWSU accepts without any doubt that everyone is good, but each one has certain specialities. In the process of self-evaluation, one must be able to discover one's own special abilities and employ those as tools of self-change and social service. This way, one can experience the best in one's potential and thus have a feeling of fulfilment.

Another important way of developing self-satisfaction in one's path of growth in value education is how far one has developed good wishes for and goodwill towards everyone. This requires the intent to be good in own self and to do good to everyone. This will be possible if we keep in mind that evil in others does not dissuade us from the good and from doing good. We must be able to listen to the voice of good conscience, silence or divine reasons. Thus, self-evaluation is the best way to gauge the success of moral education programmes.

Important Considerations

The Brahma Kumaris Ishwariya Vishwa Vidyalaya gives due considerations to the obstacles in value education. The institution is aware of the stumbling blocks in value education such as one's own 'Samskaras', vitiated atmosphere at home, school and places of work, morally polluted atmosphere of the society as a whole, 'Tamasik', food, bad company, wrong uses of information including literature related with sex and violence, weak will, personal ambition, apathy and the negative traits of parents. The institution, therefore, works to remove such obstackles as given above through counselling as well as day-to-day guidance. It imparts value education to parents as well as children through Raj Yoga Meditation. It also enlightens them on the necessity of having good which is more conducive to moral education and spiritual well-being. Students are dissuaded from taking alcoholic drinks and intoxicating drugs. Benefits of vegetarian foods are explained to the students. In short, it is stressed that we must have right type of values and attitudes as well as positive thinking and purity of emotions. In this regard, the institution emphasizes that spirituality is different from religion. The focus of spirituality is on universal values and on practices of positive thinking. It does not emphasise any type of prayers and rituals or worships of different kinds. The spirituality takes in its embrace people of all religions and even those who are atheists.

13

J. KRISHNAMURTI'S RISHI VALLEY SCHOOL

Experienced Approach to Value Education

—MULK RAJ CHILANA

Philosophical Basis

The Rishi Valley School (RVS) is a residential institution affiliated to ISC Board. Its activities reflect philosophy of education of Jiddu Krishnamurti (K). The students of the school take SLC examination at X, and Plus Two Examination at standard XII based on the curriculum set by the Board. The programmes and activities of the school are inspired by the educational philosophy of K, a well-known thinker and philosopher of our times. According to K, "Education is not merely a matter of training the mind; its purpose is not to produce mere scholars..., but integrated men and women." Freedom is the major key to achieve the objectives of K's philosophy through education. He holds "There must be absolute freedom from orthodox or traditional movements, there must be total freedom, absolute freedom, from all sense of nationalities, racial prejudices, religious beliefs and faiths." If one is not capable of doing this with honesty and integrity, it is better to keep away from this place. Essentially, one has the insight to see that knowledge is the enemy of man. The intention of the school obviously is to awaken the intelligence of the child. The school environment and teacher must help the child to flower in goodness. It is also the intention of the school to develop global outlook of the child rather than limiting him to narrower considerations. This naturally requires "an atmosphere of freedom and responsibility, a spirit of enquiry without bias and a concern for man and environment being integral to the scheme of education." The significant features of K's educational philosophy, therefore, emerge to be education of the total human being; inculcation in children a love for nature and respect for all forms of life; creation of an atmosphere of love, order, freedom without either fear or licence, avoidance from conditioning the child in any type of either religious dogma or political or social prejudices and teaching without the motive of reward or comparison.

Main Objectives

The major aim of education, according to K, is "freedom from the self". He considers this as the true function of everyman. In order to achieve this objective, it is expected that a school shapes the child into a good human being. The system of education also emphasises search for the truth in the real sense. K recommends to the student to read the book of life. The book he stresses is 'You' i.e. the child himself. He says "You are that book. It is not printed by any publisher. It is not for sale. You can't go to any analyst because his book is the same as yours." In order to achieve this objective, K advises 'Look into Yourself'. This means that apart from the physical existence, one has to see the contradictions also in oneself. This will lead to understanding of conflicts in the self. Thus, the emphasis is on understanding disorder in oneself. This will lead to understanding of the order. For achieving this objective, K advises the development of 'Religious Mind'. To develop this mind, one has to take care that this is not the ritualistic mind but it is the mind which is free. This mind does not undertake practices as suggested by others. With this mind the book of self is to be studied. The objective of this education is also to abhor one's dependence on any type of 'Authority', may it be a priest, a philosopher or a group. K also suggests an understanding of the relationships in action. He mentions about the significance of seeing how fears arise. He also emphasises that it is possible to be free from fears. For this, it is necessary not to run away, but to observe, to look, to listen and to understand what the book is saying. At this juncture, he considers time as very significant dimension of life. The relation of time and thought must also be determined. Emphasising the significance of meditation, he defines it as stopping of time and so his advice is 'not to be caught in time'. This will lead to freedom from self.

Value Frame

The school does not believe in any sort of prescription of values. It strongly goes against conditioning of any type. However, among the values emerging in the philosophy of K, the most important is 'knowing the self'. He emphasises reading of the book of life. He is of the view that without reading that book carefully and patiently one can never be able to do anything worthwhile. K also reiterates the need for an individual to change the society. According to him "Society is corrupt, immoral. There is a great deal of poverty, injustice and so on. Any serious man would be concerned with things as they are in the world at present, with all the chaos, corruption, war...." The society in which we live is brought about by each one of us, by our parents, grand parents and so on. K also mentions the need for peace in the world. War, in his opinion, is the greatest crime. Removal of the fear is, according to him, the most needed value. He feels that in order to bring change in the society, first of all, a student must be able to read the book i.e. himself. But the student must also be able to understand the society to which he and his parents have the responsibility for its development in the present form. In order to do so, the school must be able to develop a student into a 'Firsthand Person' and not a secondhand human being who is influenced by the thoughts of others. Thus, the value frame of K though not specifically elaborated, includes a search for truth, peace, good conduct, love and non-violence.

Learning Methods

The school practises experiential approach to the realisation of values of life in an open learning climate. In order to achieve the objectives of value education, methods of open discussions and dialogues are encouraged. There is no prescription for students to follow and every one is encouraged to question, to investigate in order to realise the values. This is done to make students free from emotional thinking and producing human minds that are objective, honest and have integrity in words and deeds. An open and frank dialogue between the teacher and the students serves as a means of value inculcation. The dialogue is taken as a form of communication in which questions and answers continue till a question is left without an answer. Thus, the question is suspended between two persons involved in the process of questioning and answering. This is, in fact, a form of dialogue in which an investigation reaches a certain point of intensity and depth which then has a quality which thought can never reach. Another strategy is avoidance of value prescription and direct teaching. In order to practise the cooperative methods of learning and self-introspection, K stresses the importance of the art of listening, the art of observing and the art of learning. According to him, "Listening implies not to interpret what the book is saying. Just observe it as you would observe a cloud. You don't do anything about the cloud, about palm leaves swaying in the wind or the beauty of the sunset; you can't alter it." He atresses the cultivation of mind which is aware and awake. About the art of learning, he says "Man is never free from the known—so our learning becomes mechanical. The art of learning implies something totally different. Learning means enquiry into the limits of knowledge and moving." Thus, the learning methods should revolve around the active participation of students and teachers. There is emphasis on objective thinking and conditioning is avoided. There is no consideration for readymade answers. Students are encouraged to be creaters of values and discoverers of truth rather than being passive recipients and blind followers.

Major Activities

Besides providing a learning environment conducive to realization of values and use of strategies like dialogues and discussions, RVS conducts experimental sessions for students to create an awareness about self and the world around them. There is emphasis on objective thinking and sharing of experiences. The RVS also has a Study Centre in which there is ample literature by J. Krishnamurti. There is also multi media learning material. The study centre is regarded as a place of learning, austere living and inward discipline. The students have to work without a Guru, without a leader and without a formal system of education. All this is done through questioning, doubting, investigating and drawing one's own conclusions about the realities of life. Besides the students, the study centre is open for the common people of the society. The atmosphere of the school also provides a unique opportunity for development of self. The institution is full of trees, birds and the beauty of nature. There is quietness all around, external beauty, tranquality and silence, emphasis is laid on inner beauty and love. Love and compassion are pursued as the means for the flowering of goodness in an individual. The school environment discourages cramming which leads to captivity of the mind. Competition is completely avoided. There is continuous emphasis on awakening of the mind.

Teacher's Role

In order to impart value education the teacher's role is that of mediator and facilitator rather than that of the dispenser of knowledge. He has to develop himself not only as a good questioner, but he should also learn to give explanations which are open-ended. This will enable the students to get an opportunity to explore and find out. In this way, the teacher has to assume the role of co-learner in the classroom. For dialogue, the teacher has to be a good communicator. More than his questions, his answers should lead to further questioning by students. He will be a successful teacher if he can encourage the spirit of enquiry among students by questioning answers more rather than by answering the questions. In the RVS, teachers make deliberate efforts to create a facilitative and participative learning environment. The teacher is a sort of manager of a variety of learning resources rather than himself being the sole resource of learning. Thus, the teacher helps and guides the students in their search for the mission of life through exploration and enquiry rather than by providing readymade answers. K condemns mere acquisition of knowledge which leads the mind to become dull. Such acquisition dictates conduct of life and, therefore, limits experience; whereas learning is limitless.

Some Implications

In the Rishi Valley School, realization rather than preaching of values is given more importance. There is more emphasis on value-charged school environment which is created by providing a lot of functional autonomy to teachers and learning autonomy to students. This enables students to discover their values instead of being indoctrinated into the same. Some universal values like truth, love, peace and non-violence are considered essential part of education, but the emphasis is more on experiencing these values by the students, rather than these being prescribed in the curriculum and reinforced through the lectures of the teachers. Similarly, proper behaviour by students is considered very important for creating a good society. The teacher in such a school atmosphere assumes the role of manager of learning environment. He is the mediator as well as facilitator of learning. An atmosphere of free dialogue between students and teachers is praise-worthy, but this requires exposure of the teachers to better interactive learning strategies. For success of value realization, strategies as practised in RVS, there is a need for special creed of teachers who can assume the roles of being educators, guides, co-learners with students, contingency managers and objective thinkers. This would require teachers who are continuously growing in their profession and are fully vigilant about the needs of the students. They have to be fully aware of the individual needs of the students. They have to be fully aware of the individual needs as well as social problems of the human beings. Their skill lies in successfully fulfilling both the objectives, and not accomplishing one at the cost of the other. Thus, experimental approach to value education is an·admirable way to develop universal values which will become an integral part of the life of an individual.

14

VALUE-ORIENTED EDUCATION IN BANASTHALI VIDYAPITH

Behavioural Spirituality and Balance

—MULK RAJ CHILANA

Basis for Values

Banasthali Vidyapith is a unique institution for education and training of girls. It was started in 1927 by Pandit Hira Lal Shastri, a distinguished social reformer and educationist. The Vidyapith aims at full and balanced development of the personality of every student. Its goal is named as 'Panchmukhi Shikshan'. From the very beginning, the institution started experimentation for balanced development of five aspects of education, viz., physical, intellectual, moral, aesthetic and practical. The Vidyapith has students from primary to post-graduate classes. Its school section was earlier affiliated to the Board of Secondary Education, Rajasthan and the college section was attached to the University of Rajasthan. However, efforts of the Vidyapith succeeded for getting autonomy as it got the status of Deemed University on October 25, 1983. This provided an opportunity to the institution for having freedom to experiment and innovate.

Major Institutional Objectives

The constitution of the Vidyapith lays down that one of the its premier aims is the synthesis of science and spirituality. This includes striking a balance between material and spiritual values. Spirituality, according to the Vidyapith, is not attaining 'Moksha'. Rather, it focuses on developing a moral sense which can be derived by emphasizing the spirit of universal oneness. Thus, universal oneness is considered as 'behaviour spirituality'. The Vidyapith recognises that overuse of science and technology in the modern world is posing a great problem for value education. It, therefore, tries to inculcate values in the students by developing particular ethos in all its activities in the classroom, during the cocurricular activities, in the hostel life and mother such programmes outside the classroom. The emphasis is on the ethos of peace, mutual love and consideration, proper behaviour and such moral values as lead to realisation of the spirit embodied in 'Simple Living and High Thinking'.

Value Education Approaches

The Vidyapith is of the view that value orientation should not primarily be a separate activity like any other content. It should form an integral part of one's personality. It believes that development of values will generally depend on two things; first is the ethos in which one lives and the second is the persons with whom one comes into contact. It feels that value orientation is affected by four factors; one's 'Samaskaras', Family Ethos, Social Ethos and Ethos of the Educational Institution where one is getting eduction. Thus, role of the educational institution is to provide proper atmosphere for the growth and development of an individual who is eager to receive the total ethos of the institution in conformity with the aforesaid views on values. The teachers take due care for planning of the programme of celebrating festivals and other activities like games, cultural programmes and dramas, besides normal instruction in the classroom. They don't consider value orientation as a separate programme like any other content, but an integral part of education. This enables the Institution to exhort the teachers to themselves practise the values in their thoughts, speech, actions and emotions.

Major Content Areas

From the very beginning Banasthali Vidyapith has stressed the need for study of Indian culture and nationalism. It is of firm view that for the country to become truly free, it is necessary to acquaint the students with Indian culture. It considers nationalism as an attitude of oneness, a sense of belongingness to the nation and affinity to the country. It is emphasised that nation is not merely a geo-political concept, but essentially a cultural concept. The Indian view of life is also given due importance as far as the content of value orientation programme is concerned. In this connection, it gives due consideration to cultural roots of the nation in the Hindu view of life. It does give importance to the study of the development in the country through centuries which has been dynamic and open. Thus, it gives ample regards to the Hindu spirit of adaptation and assimilation. The five characteristics of Indian culture emphasised by the *Vidyapith* are 'Totality', 'Depth', 'Tolerance or generosity', 'Receptivity to learn' and 'Avoiding extremes to maintain balance'. This balanced view of life has been accepted as expressed in the four 'Purusharthas' i.e. 'Dharma', 'Artha', 'Kama' and 'Moksha'. The Vidyapith considers it equally important to include value 'system which is characterised by the aspiration of modern society. These values include admiration for modern science and technology, egalitarianism, economic justice, socio-religious and cultural freedom and secularism.

Specific Methods Followed

The methodology of value orientation includes activities for students with emphasis on model behaviour. The teachers and students have to be vigilant to ensure that general behaviour of the students is intelligent and based on mutual cooperation. It is emphasised that students should be able to discriminate as to what is the right and what is the wrong behaviour. The *Vidyapith* considers that the role of teacher is very important in this regard. The teacher should set an example for the students to emulate. Prayer constitute, a very vital programme in the *Vidyapith.* Education is considered essentially a human process for the development of values. It is felt that values have to be based on moral norms. The *Vidyapith* considers that religious and spiritual values are very important. Therefore, the emphasis is on such prayers which refer to all important religions. Thus students follow 'Sarva Dharma Prarthana' on the lines advocated by Gandhiji. Similarly, students and teachers explain quotations from almost all major religions. Obviously these prayers and quotations show respect for all and offend none. The staff and students take utmost care that religious sentiments of others are not hurt. In activities like prayers and cultural programmes, the Institution encourages voluntary participation rather than compulsion to attend.

Informal Integral Evaluation

The methods of evaluation are informal and integral rather than formal. They are not limited to the end-of-the-year summative evaluation. The behaviour of students is watched by teachers and they are corrected whenever deviation from the norm is found. The emphasis is on helping students to be good individuals and good citizens. Efforts are made to check such tendencies which disturb the family life and social ethos. However, the course on Indian heritage is examined through written tests.

Not Education Alone

Development of integrated and balanced personality is the main aim of education in Banasthali Vidyapith. So in the development of five-fold education, moral education occupies a very significant place. Since education is the development of total personality, it is evident that right development implies 'Right Values'. The Vidyapith system accepts that values arise from one's attitude. This attitude is, in turn, the result of one's efforts, one's environment and one's inherited 'Samaskaras'. It has strong belief that proper efforts and environment can definitely modify an individual's inherited 'Samaskaras'. Therefore, role of education is considered significant in the formation of values. Apart from the role of value education, the university authorities believe that there is need for substantial change in the society. They are of the opinion, that looking at the broad social situation there is a lot of deterioration. The indiscrete multiplication of wants is the basic cause for increase in the desires. This has happened because of the misuse of modern technology in producing a large variety of unnecessary goods and services. The *Vidyapith* is, therefore, of the opinion that unless this social background is taken care of and properly regulated, substantial change in the society may not be possible only through education.

15

RAMAKRISHNA INSTITUTE OF MORAL AND SPIRITUAL EDUCATION

Value Orientation is the Mission

—MULK RAJ CHILANA

A Unique Institute

The Ramakrishna Institute of Moral and Spiritual Education is unique for its being solely dedicated to the cause of moral and spiritual values. Because of its pioneering and valuable work in this field, it has earned the distinction for singular devotion to help in the development of ideal human beings. Founded on the philosophy of Sri Ramakrishan Paramhans, the twin goals of self-realisation and service to the mankind appear to be major guidelines for the organisation. Of course, the institute undertakes a variety of services such as education, medical assistance, cultural and religious programmes, rural development and relief work and helping people suffering from natural calamaties like earthquakes, floods and epidemics. An important consideration in all its activities is to respond to the clarion call of Swami Vivekanand who wanted to rebuild the nation on the laudable values of the ancient culture mixed with the relevant need of today which is characterised by scientific and technological advancement. Thus the lofty principles of Swami Vivekanand are a blend of the ancient wisdom of the past as well as the modern needs of the country. In order to carry out the work on the aforesaid lines the Ramakrishna Mission realized that education is the most appropriate medium. Further, the Institution feels that training of teachers is the most important need for effective value education. In prusuance of this goal, the foundation stone of Ramakrishna Institute of Moral and Spiritual Education

(RIMSE) was laid in 1968 and the building was ready in 1974. This institution has an all-India character for the purpose of giving moral and spiritual education to teachers, both at pre-service and in-service levels. In addition to training of teachers, students at school and college levels are also covered. They also undertake activities like training of public in general and organisation of seminar and other such activities which lead to intensive thinking and research in order to promote value orientation.

Experiences and Experiments

The Ramakrishna Ashram Mysore which guides the activities of RIMSE has a very long experience in organising varied activities including special experiment extension work in the field of moral and spiritual education. Their programme of 'Retreats' attracts men of great repute for upgrading their consciousness. 'Retreat' means to withdraw the mind from the outer world and to look within in order to understand one's nature, to dwell on different aspects of divinity, to introspect on one's role in the world and to prepare oneself for discharging one's responsibilities. The duration of these retreats varies from 3 to 10 days to meet the needs and demands of different groups of participants. The success of these programmes also attracts a large number of teachers. This has led to requests from many schools and other educational institutions to arrange similar programmes for their students as well as teachers. Some national and state level educationists as well as eminent people from the areas of science, technology, humanities and arts have also gone through this experiment. They evince great interest in the programme and offer support and cooperation for similar activities. The experience of Ramakrishna Ashram shows similar results in the field of medical health and relief work. As far as moral and spiritual development is concerned, the Ashram organises direct activities in their own schools as well as extends help to all others who approach them.

Value-Related Activities

Since the formal operationalization of RIMSE on Ist July, 1974, the Institute engages in organisation of several courses and pursues a number of related activities. The courses include a 10-month B.Ed.

course affiliated to the University of Mysore with compulsory content-cum-methodology in moral and spiritual education and a diploma in moral and spiritual education of two months duration for in-service teachers of secondary schools of the state of Karnataka. 'Retreats' for general public are organised twice a year for the duration of five days each. National integration camps for boys are held for the duration of ten days. 'Retreat' for the Ramakrishna Vidyashala is a regular feature of RIMSE. Their extension activities are organised through Vivekananda Tarun Sangh which is a Sunday School for local primary and secondary school students. They also go to the local community for extending help and assistance and to provide relief work. All the courses mentioned above are fully residential. Among the most prominent principles promoted during the activities are religious tolerance, dignity of labour, individual discipline, inner peace, self-reliance and social harmony.

B.Ed. with Values

RIMSE has the distinction of being the only institution so far in the country which has introduced, in its curriculum, compulsory instructions for moral and spiritual education, both in the content and methodology. The major objectives of the B.Ed. course is to provide value education in theory and practice to those who opt for the teaching profession. This programme is being truly followed as recommended by Kothari Commission. The course also impresses upon the young teacher-trainees the importance of national unity and it inspires them to get interested in the rich cultural heritage of the country. They also get to know the problems of Indian society such as social barriers, environmental destruction, hampering prejudices and devastating effect of caste and self-interest at the cost of social development. Besides, they work on the positive directions to develop in the trainees healthy attitude towards life, sensitivity towards environment and spirit of service to the community. In fact, the course endeavours to develop global outlook and sense of belongingness to the whole humanity. The B.Ed. course is affiliated to the University of Mysore and it differs from other colleges as far as compulsory study of moral spiritual education is concerned, both in content as well as methodology. The content course includes the study of major religions of the world and stresses on the essential unity in all these religions so as to foster a sense of brotherhood of man and fatherhood of God. Due focus is given on the social problems which hinder moral education such as drug addiction, drinking, corruption, environmental pollution and decline in moral values. The students are given special training in preparation of suitable instructional materials. Daily routine of the course starts with a morning prayer and it includes many activities like meditation, yoga classes, 'shramdan', class lectures, independent studies, music and bhajans and spors and games. These activities promote desire for excellence as spirit of partiotism, sense of equality and dignity of labour and spiritual upliftment.

For In-Service Teachers

The success of B.Ed. course in RIMSE has moved the Education Department of Karnataka State to seek their help in in-service education of teachers. The Government of Karnataka deputes 200 teachers every year for a two-month Diploma Course in Moral and Spiritual Education. In each of these four courses of two-month duration, the purpose is to enlarge the outlook of teachers and to stimulate them for thinking on different dimensions of moral and spiritual training of students. The training programmes include regular discourses and discussions on prominent world religions and their common universal teachings regarding the moral and spiritual path to be followed for the well-being and progress of mankind. India's cultural heritage is given special importance so that glorious past of the country is properly understood by students. Similarly, biographies of great men include saints and scientists as well as philosophers and statesmen to provide inspiration to students to emulate their example.

Methodology of moral education is also given due importance. Special lectures are arranged by expert guest scholars. Periodical screening of films of moral and spiritual values is also done. There is a very close coordination of in-service teachers with the faculty and students of the B.Ed. wing of RIMSE.

Covering the Youth

Apart from the teachers at the pre-service and in-service levels. RIMSE organises programmes for college and school students from different parts of the country through 'Retreats' and 'National

Integration Camps'. The duration of these course camps varies from 8 to 10 days. These programmes aim to impress upon the young minds the greatness of all religions and the need for tolerance and acceptance of the views of others. The importance of moral values and character is also stressed during the programmes. The young students engage in social service and go to villages to serve the community and the poor at the time of natural calamities. The youth is also helped in understanding important needs of the country like national integration, preservation of environment and promotion of human rights. The teaching and learning methods followed during these summer 'Retreats' and national integration camps include classroom lectures, discussion on subjects of national importance and cultural heritage of India. They also provide training in *yogasanas*.

Other Related Activities

The other activities of the Institute include extension activities, organisation of national seminars and helping the community in the event of natural calamities. The RIMSE also provides extension services to school children of several other institutions. The children from primary and high schools visit the Institute on Sundays to participate in the community prayer and to get instructions on moral education. The Institute has a special section in their library devoted to children of different age-groups. They are also shown films and given opportunities for social service. A national seminar on Value Orientation was also held by RIMSE. It discussed several important issues related to value orientation in teacher education, elementary education, secondary and higher education and technical education. It also discussed basic aims of value-oriented education and research in value-oriented education. The Institute undoubtedly has men of talent and experience with a high sense of service. They are quite competent to work for the cause of value education in the country.

16

HUMAN VALUES
A Voyage from I to We

—ANTONIO CRAXI

A doubt may arise when we do not take into account the following fundamental principle: knowledge lies within each one of us and where there is purity, it manifests itself naturally. Can we find anything purer than a child's heart, whose thirst for love and knowledge has no limit? We had to overcome our mental doubts and fears, in order to communicate with the children.

Comprehension is immediate through such heart-to-heart communion, and the precious seeds of values can grow and blossom in the rich soil of their hearts.

We started by setting up an instrument that would help these fundamental values inherent to human personality manifest themselves. We had to prepare a kind of ABC of spirituality, a reference for one's daily living, that could foster human nature through a clear comprehension of human values.

In this modern era, the means of communication are innumerable and highly sophisticated; nevertheless, the principle of teaching is, and will always be, one and the same. Today, just as yesterday, the teacher goes through illustrations and examples taken out from nature, in order to teach the letters of the alphabet: A for apple, B for banana, C for cat etc. We followed the same idea, putting together illustrations and abstract philosophical concepts. This has been the fundamental inspiration for setting up the exhibition on "Human Values".

We met many artists who, with great generosity and good will,

Chairman European Foundation for Human Values, Ferme Des ifs Chemen du Buguet-14600, Honfleur-France.

offered freely their talents for concretising this project. It took two years, from 1985 to 1987, to do so. Finally, the exhibition took place and was presented for the first time in Milan, on the 4th of November 1987.

It went on through several cities in Italy, in France, in Brazil and in India. The President of Italian Republic conferred on it his high patronage and the Italian Minister of Education contributed to its spreading to the schools. 75000 pupils have visited it and many seminars have taken place in order to form the guides, whose voluntary service is invaluable.

It is important here to explain that the method that is used for communicating the values to the children, is entirely based on the *Maieutics*, the art of dialogue as proposed by Socrates. Step by step and through a series of questions and answers, the children realise the very truth Plato used to describe. They "deliver" their own Self, as Socrates put it.

The volume *The Human Values—A Voyage from I to We* has been published in Italian, French, English, Portuguese and Greek (Edizioni Persona della Fondazione Europea Divulgazione Valori Umani—Via S. Francesco d'Assisi, 45-Ponte-Vecchio di Magenta-20013 - Italy). This book contains 81 illustrations of the Exhibition "The Human Values", together with their text, commentary, exercise, test of personality, teaching objective. This book is an excellent instrument, and together with the exhibition, it represents a precious aid for the diffusion of Human Values among the youth, and it allows us to perform our institutional duties.

The Exhibition "The Human Values" consists of 81 posters, four-colour process, 100 × 150 cm each, printed on coated paper—180gr. Plastic coated, 500 exemplaries printed, in Italian and English language. These posters represent, through each painting, illustration and graphic representation, different philosophical concepts based on the five fundamental Human Values: truth, right action, peace, love and non-violence.

It is meant for Primary and Secondary school students (from 7 to 15 years), but anyone may derive benefit from it whatever age or condition.

Human Values and Education

The word "Education" has its root in the Latin word: Exducere" or, "to bring out". True education lies in bringing forth the human values in man, thus allowing the blossoming of his personality. The great Greek philosopher Socrates defines education as the art of shaping the intelligence and forming the character. Thus, he used to make the noble youth of Athens excell in the practice of public as well as private virtues.

Sathya Sai Baba says:

> "Education must instill the fundamental human values; it must broaden the vision, to include the entire world and all mankind. Education must equip man to live happily, without making others unhappy, to evaluate things, pleasure and possessions correctly and without prejudice, and fix one's attention ever on the highest and the most precious achivement of all, the spiritual victory. The spiritual stream must flow in the heart as the source and spring of all endeavour."

And about the actual educational systems:

> "Any system of education that does not help discriminate between right and wrong, that does not instill fear of sin and love for God, train you in the codes of humility and reverence, widen the horizon of your wonder, encourage you to worshipfully serve your parents and inspire you to dedicate your skills and attainments to the progress of your family, your village, community, country, language and nation, stands condemned."

This type of education, such as it was existing thousands of years ago, has disappeared, hence the urge to restore it today. *Modern education does not transform the individual, it merely informs and very often, deforms the minds of the youth.* Based on notions and informations, it totally ignores the values and the human personality.

It is our experience that all the concepts illustrated through the exhibition "The Human Values" are easily grasped by the children who immediately focus their attention, and develop their concentration together with their faculty of intuition. The deep interest they show in the matter proves on its own the incredible possibilities lying within this didactic means.

The children themselves sow the seeds for right action, by the practice of proper reasoning; they develop their will power and it becomes easy for them to follow the dictates of their conscience.

This way, through the knowledge of Human Values, education contributes in forming true men, who are able to face life and its many difficulties, making it meaningful.

The Human Values are as follows: truth, right action, peace, love and non-violence. Through their practice, the human personality will blossom in its different aspects: physical, mental, psychic, intellectual and spiritual.

These values belong essentially to man, no other creature in this vast creation can claim such heritage. When we refer to 'man', we mean a creature with a human body, a mind, an intellect and a spirit. The latter being the basis of everything, the life-giving element that allows the manifestation of life in all these aspects.

The values spring forth from the spirit of which they are a projection and to which they go back at the end of the voyage from "I" to "We". In this lies the whole idea presented in the Exhibition: "The Human Values".

The graphical presentation of the values, a rainbow in the form of a heart, illustrates the following concept: "The human values are the priceless treasure deposited from time immemorial in the bottom of my heart". They are nothing else than the colourful projection of our inner light....

Let us take the first value, that is truth. The truth here is a transcendental value, it is the answer to the following question: "Who am I? Where do I come from? What is my destination?" Sages and perfect beings at many periods of human history have given us many hints. They have told us how to proceed in this enquiry: "Who am I?", in order to help us understand our true nature, as well as the nature of the world.

When we say for instance: "I am, I do, I think, I want etc." let us ask ourselves "Who is this I" who always appears in our expression, at all ages, under all circumstances, all life through. The effort one makes in answering such questions is the final goal of human life. When I assert myself thus: "I am Paul", I declare that Paul is the name that has been given to the "I". But before receiving this name, Paul, who am I? After the pronoun 'I' comes the possessive 'mine'—I and mine are always linked. When I say for instance: "This is my arm" I do not say that I am the arm, but that the arm belongs to me, I am the owner of this arm.

When I proceed, saying: "This is my stomach, this is my mind, this is my intelligence etc." I declare that I am different from all these things, that they belong to me. When I further declare: "This is my body". Am I this body? No! This body belongs to me, it is an instrument which I use in order to make the experience of the world around me.

The question remains: "Who am I, if am I not this body?"

Each world expresses a reality, the science that studies the formation of sounds and words is called *semantic*. Within the verb the whole universe lies. Words are very powerful, as they contain a hidden and deeper meaning. Behind their expression lies the essential truth, what is left after all the words have been said and all the thoughts expressed IS the truth.

When I further declare: "This is my soul" for instance, I assert that the soul belongs to me, that I am Its owner. But who am I, I am not the body, not the mind, not the emotions, not the intelligence, not the soul. The question remains: "Who is this I, the owner of all these instruments, this everpresent I?" The answer is simple: "I am I" beyond words and beyond oral expression, I exist, I am the truth. Only the experience of this truth will give me the ultimate answer.

This illuminating experience is the goal of any spiritual endeavour, it is meant for all men, nothing is more important than this.

Each and every flash of truth illuminating our heart will bring us closer to the following truth: "Light is my very nature, it is divine energy, it pervades everything. Lost in the darkness of ignorance, I didn't know it. Now, I can realise it."

Truth put into practice is the right action. It is only through such an action that the energy of love can manifest itself. Within man we define it as 'Conscience', as compassion, tolerance, in other words: "altruism". It is an all expansive energy that projects through the various aspects of human personality. Such light illuminates the way of life. It is the same energy that sustains the entire universe and pervades creation. In the words of the great poet Dante Alighieri: *"Amor che muove il sole e le altre stelle...."—"Love that makes the sun and all the stars move...."*

When this love reaches the mountain top from which one can perceive the infinite horizon of the human heart, then the identification with all creation, the feeling of perfect unity will annihilate the limits contained in the "I" and in the "mine" and take us to the "we", the step to universal love, to the last value, the destination, the truth that is beyond any expression.

The greatest need in modern society is to get good people, the greater their number, the more human, society will be. The entire humanity is linked by the bond of love. When this chain of love breaks under the pressure of hatred, men are dragged to lower levels, they become animals and even demons. Today we have to face the tearing apart of the social tissue, eaten by the moths of envy, jealously, anger and hatred.

A human form is not the sign of humanity. To deserve to be called a "man" the practice of human values is essential. Without a spritual vision of the world, man will never reach out to the first rank in creation, that is his heritage.

Our task is, therefore, to help by any means, under any circumstances, more and more human beings, to become aware of this precious heritage, that is their very birthright. Nothing is more urgent today.

17

EDUCATION AT RISHI VALLEY

—KRISHNAMURTHI FOUNDATION, MADRAS

History

Rishi Valley School had its inception in the 1920s when Sri J. Krishnamurthi and Dr. Annie Besant arranged to buy 200 acres of land in rural Andhra Pradesh. The school proper was established on its present campus in the Thettu Valley in 1930. Madanapalle, the nearest small town, is about 16 kms away while Bangalore lies 210 kms to the west.

The area is chronically drought prone, being part of the Rayalseema region where the annual rainfall of about 60 cms is sharply reduced in bad years.

The population consists largely of marginal farmers with small holdings on which rain-fed crops are grown; many are daily wage earners working as agricultural labour. Dairy keeping, rearing of sheep and goats are also practised.

After sixty years the campus is shaded with mature trees. There is a modern dairy with around 50 milking cows; an organic vegetable farm; fruit orchards with mangoes, saphotas and guavas.

Biogas plants and solar heaters partially fulfil the energy requirements on campus.

Rishi Valley School

RVS is a residential school with about 350 students drawn from various parts of India and from countries abroad. Admission is selective: about 12% of applicants are accepted. The student body is

Krishna Murthi Foundation, Madras.

chosen for character and talents in addition to academic excellence. The school gives active consideration to candidates from minority communities and from families involved in social work who have difficulties educating their children. Our students body is by and large drawn from the urban centres of India; there are about 10% non-resident Indians and occasionally students from Japan, Australia and North America.

We have a large and highly dedicated faculty (45 teachers for 350 students), whose members are unusually well qualified in their subjects. Many have done post-graduate work, ten members of our staff have Ph.D. degrees, and four are Indian Institute of Technology graduates. A great deal of effort has gone into developing original curricular material in the humanities and the sciences. Dr. Shirali, Principal and Head of Mathematics, is a leading member of the International Mathematic Olympiad Committee and in-charge of training students selected to represent India. Facilities at the school include an outstanding library, an extensive collection of audio-video aids, an active computer centre and a Junior School Mathematics Resource Centre designed under the supervision of Sri P.K. Srinivasan, a distinguished teacher of mathematics who recently won a national award for promoting science in India.

National Examinations are taken at the end of Grade X (ICSE) and again at the Grade XII (ISC). The last two years at the Rishi Valley School form a separate programmes for which admissions are open and students are screened anew as candidates. A General Studies programme at the senior level (Grades XI and XII) is intended to extend students intellectual horizons, and also to heighten their awareness of environmental issues.

We place a high premium on academic excellence as well as on overall development of our students within a non-competitive framework. Our concern is to teach students to become aware of themselves and of their human and natural environment. Our results in the examination are well above the national average and graduating students find places in some of the best educational institutions in India as well as abroad.

Rishi Valley School is part of the Rishi Valley Education Centre, which also runs a Rural Education Centre, seven free schools for poor children from the local villages and engages in rural development activities including afforestation, alternative energy, medical care and programmes for rural craft such as pottery.

Our teachers and our students learn to share these responsibilities and are encouraged to participate in some of the programmes.

Since Rishi Valley School is situated in one of the poorest districts of rural India, our concern over the years has been to extend the already established educational base in ways that would bring multiple benefits to the countryside and its populations.

Ours is a holistic approach inspired by J. Krishnamurti's philosophy of education. Four basic ideas underline the extension work we have undertaken: to turn a public school into a resource centre for the countryside. Secondly, to establish a network of small and medium sized schools that can support each other through joint programmes. Thirdly, to make the curriculum relevant to the geographical and cultural area in which our schools are located. And lastly, to anchor the educational process in programmes that lead eventually to the regeneration of the landscape in this drought-prone district consisting of degraded forests, denuded hills and small valleys. In due course our hope is that the schools we establish and interact with will become the impetus for the establishment and growth of village commons where fruit-bearing trees, fodder, and fuel will be shared equally by all the families of the village.

RURAL EDUCATION AT RISHI VALLEY

History and Organizational Aims

The Rishi Valley Rural Education Centre was set up on the campus of the Rishi Valley Education Centre in 1976 with 14 acres of land attached to it. A boarding school (The Rishi Valley School), one of the leading public schools in the country, with 350 students drawn from the urban centres of India and a highly educated faculty; a dairy; vegetable garden and other infrastructure to maintain this school, were already in place.

In 1984, with the encouragement and active help of several teachers from the Rishi Valley School, we began an involvement with the countryside that has rapidly developed into an integrated rural educational programme which is fast becoming a model for several schools in Andhra Pradesh.

The several district components of the programme are described below.

The Institutions at REC

The following institutions are located on the campus of REC:

(i) *Rishivanam* is a free day school for 100 children of the immediate neighbourhood. We provide a health care, a free midday meal and clothes to all the children of the school. Even though it is an experimental school, students are prepared for the Andhra matriculation examination. Academic training is supplemented by a rich programme in crafts, music, puppetry and new techniques of farming like permaculture and athletics.

(ii) *Rural Health Centre*: A programme which caters to the needs of the students and the surrounding villagers. The medical officer of the Rishi Valley School attends to the needs of the patients during morning hours five days a week.

(iii) *Curriculum Development Cell*: Innovative educational programmes, relevant to the rural needs of Andhra Pradesh, have been developed. The material has been gathered together into a package catering to the total educational needs of a primary school. The kit is suitable for all formal as well as non-formal schools including Balwadis, Nursery Schools, Primary Schools.

The educational kit promotes self-learning on the part of the students and enables teachers to deal with their subject matter in a well-organized, graded manner. The kit has been especially designed and tested for first generation learners, and has sufficient flexibility of approach and richness of content built into it to make it suitable for use in all primary schools. The aim of the kit is to enable students to actively participate in the learning process. The kit will contain the following items:

Telugu Language Teaching Programme

A graded step by step programme which includes skill building and evaluation components built into it. Includes (1) The material gradually builds reading and writing skills through controlled use of vocabulary, starting from the level of preliminary exercises.

Traditional and local stories are retold to hold the child's attention; (2) Language games to reinforce concepts already learnt; (3) Activity cards for mime, puppetry and drama to encourage oral skills; (4) Self-evaluation worksheets that test the level of learning; (5) Supplementary reading material; (6) A manual for language teachers.

Mathematics Programme

With the help of Shri P.K. Srinivasan, a nationally known mathematics teacher, we have developed an elaborate programme for teaching mathematics. The curriculum is augmented by worksheets and teaching aids aimed at leading the child through every step of conceptual learning. The attempt has been to make theoretical concepts in mathematics concrete. Includes (1) Graded cards that lay our foundation concepts; (2) Games that encourages familiarity with numbers and improve computing skills; (3) Ideas for mathematics projects; (4) A manual for teachers of mathematics explaining the use of the kit.

Environmental Studies

We are trying to get away from a rigid academic approach to environmental studies. We encourage learning in this area through direct looking, interviewing, discussing and doing. The learning process is, therefore, a guided one, and the emphasis is on group projects. The approach combines science and social studies together in meaningful ways. Guided activities for these projects include formats that allow students to carry out a variety of surveys. Didactic Theatre, including mime and puppetry, has become a useful educational tool to convey socially relevant themes like the value of reforestation, the dangers of indiscriminate use of pesticides, proper hygiene and so on. Talented artists and writers, some of them very well known, working closely with resident staff, have contributed scripts for our kit, which includes the following materials: (1) Cards introducing students to basic concepts; (2) Information cards; (3) Experiments that students can conduct in groups; (4) Format charts for conducting surveys of various kinds; (5) Self-evaluation work materials; (6) Scripts on environmental themes especially written by eminent writers for the Rishi Valley Puppet Theatre; (7) Manuals for the use of low cost teaching aids; (8) Ideas for classroom projects on environmental studies.

Arts and Crafts Programme

Includes (1) A simple manual for teachers; and (2) A selection of action rhymes and songs.

A Teacher's Guide to Evaluating Students' Work

(iv) *Teacher Training Programme*: We have introduced a unique teacher training scheme for local youth who have school leaving certificate. Our method of training enables teachers to handle vertically grouped classes made up of students belonging to different age and ability groups. A vertically grouped class is one where children of various ages sit in the same classroom and study one or many subjects. But not every child is at the same level and need not engage in the same kind of work. Children can thus learn at their own pace. One-room schools, stocked with low cost teaching aids, and manned by a single teacher are able to meet the diverse needs of students of different ages. Teacher trainees ae taught to make low cost aids designed by experts in the field. Even primary education in rural areas tends to concentrate on abstract curricula based on text books; our efforts have been to focus the educational process on the immediate environment, and to develop the general intelligence of the student. The emphasis is on training teachers in the methods and teachniques of elementary education. Our hope is that these trained teachers will set up their own one-room schools in small villages.

Apart from the academic subjects, teachers having received training at one time or another in the following areas:

(a) permaculture; (b) book binding; (c) crafts, including textile printing, embroidery and carpentry; (d) paper mache and paper making; (e) primary health work.

Satellite Schools

The above infrastructure has enabled us to start a cluster of small schools in inaccessible villages located on land donated by the village. These are one-room schools; a teacher trained in the techniques of vertical grouping and able to handle a mixed ability group of about thirty students of varying ages manages these schools. At present we have six such schools, one of which has a craft component and in the evening doubles as a non-formal school catering to the needs of working children. The satellite schools are resource centres for their villages; they provide the following activities:

(a) adult literacy; (b) land reclamation schemes; (c) reforestation; (d) bee keeping; (e) health, hygiene and family planning; (f) puppet making.

The satellite schools are located at the following villages around the Andhra-Karnataka border:

(a)	Thettu Harijan village	30 students
(b)	Bayareddipalle village	35 students
(c)	Curralavaripalle village	35 students
(d)	Pujarivaripalle village	35 students
(e)	Eguvaboyapalle village	60 students
(f)	Chintegarikota village	26 students
(g)	Neel Bagh School	25 students

We conceived the REC as a resource centre for the countryside. All the satellite schools are linked to the REC in intricate ways: through weekly seminars for teachers where innovative educational materials are produced, through writer's workshops, sports and craft workshops, through seminars in rural development organised with the help of IRMA. The medical officer on the Rishi Valley visits all the schools from time to time.

Management and Administration

The REC is managed by Shri Padmanabha Rao, who is both headmaster and coordinator of rural activities. 4 teachers with graduate degrees and one junior teacher augment his work. Teachers from the Rishi Valley School continue to be associated with the work in the rural school.

The administrative division of the Rishi Valley Education

Centre provides the services in the area of accounts and so on.

The REC resident medical officer runs a clinic at Rishivanam and also at Neel Bagh. On an averag he treats about 120 patients per day at these rural clinics.

The Managing Committee of Rishi Valley Education Centre

Dr. Radhika Herzberger (Ph.D. University of Toronto) has worked at Rishi Valley since 1983 and is now Director. Her book on ancient Indian philosophy "Bhartrhari and the Buddhists" was published by Dr. Reidel in Holland in 1986. She is presently teaching social studies and ancient Indian history and also preparing to publish books for children in this area.

Dr. Shailesh Shirali (Ph.D. University of Texas) was educated at St. Stephens College Delhi and Ahmedabad Institute of Management. Dr. Shirali is Principal of Rishi Valley School where he also heads the department of mathematics. He has been an official coach of the Indian Olympiad team in mathematics. He is planning several publications in the area of school mathematics.

Dr. A. Kumaraswami (Ph.D. Indian Institute of Technology, Madras) is Secretary of the Rishi Valley Education Centre and head of the physics department. His extensive experience of the rural world of Andhra Pradesh is a real asset to our rural programmes.

Mr. H. Hamid (B.A. Cuttak Univerity) is headmaster of Rishi Valley School and in-charge of the geography department.

Mr. Alik Mathur (M.Ed. Harvard University) is head of the Junior and Middle School; he also teaches science and mathematics and inteacts with the teachers of rural schools.

Professor Hans Herzberger (Ph.D. Princeton University) is Professor of Philosophy at University of Toronto (Canada), who is resident half of each year at Rishi Valley.

Mr. S. Sundaram (Chartered Accountant) is Financial Manager.

Mr. S. Naidu (B.Ed. BT College, Madanapalle) is Estate Manager.

The Managing Committee also has two positions for teachers who serve one term each on a rotating basis.

Beneficiaries of the Rural Education Programme

The beneficiaries are mostly Scheduled Castes and Scheduled

Tribes. The majority of students at Rishivanam and at the satellite schools, all of which are run by the Rishi Valley Education Centre, belong to scheduled classes and scheduled tribes. Their parents are typically shepherds and marginal farmers, living in inaccessible hamlets.

Republic Character of REC's Work

Our rural programme is becoming something of a model for established educational institutions based in the rural areas that wish to extend their resources to the villages. Several NGO groups send teams to the campus to study our work with a view to transferring the structure and the curriculum to their locality. We have recently entered into an agreement with the Bhagavatullah Charitable Trust, which runs 500 schools, to train their teachers and help them set up resource centres, train teachers and also provide teaching materials around Vishakhapatnam. We have also been approched by the Centre for Environmental Education in Bangalore, which is a branch of the institution in Ahmedabad, for help in planning their clusters of schools in South India. Nagarjuna Fertilizer has also sent teams to study our approach to rural work.

Rishi Valley Publication Series

The aim of this project is to document and further advance Rishi Valley's distinctive approach to education in a village environment, including current efforts to integrate the education of boarding school student with rural activities, satellite schools, and regeneration of the earth. Our publications are designed to provide enrichment material for students from the urban middle class and those from the rural countryside, and also to reach out to other schools and to the general public with a view to testing our materials for their wider educational relevance.

Rishi Valley's educational philosophy is derived from the teachings of J. Krishnamurti and from values inherent in those teachings. Our educational priorities are to promote awareness and care for fellow human beings; to ensure excellence in academics; and to nurture a sense of beauty.

Nature Studies

Birds of Rishi Valley, by S. Rangaswami and S. Shridhar with essays and notes by several other naturalists. A richly illustrated compendium of nature lore, including a field guide and an extended study of interaction between birds and their environment also tells the story of how reforestation has led to return of many species of birds to the Valley, which now provides a rich variety of habitats for more than one hundred and fifty distinct species of birds. Fifty colour plates by eminent photographer and naturalist S. Sridhar; drawings by Gerry Balcombe.

Insects of Rishi Valley, by Rebecca Thomas. An illustrated study recording the diversity of local insect life and tracing its role in preserving the environment based on the auther's many years' experience of teaching biology in the Senior School. Using local case studies, the book will emphasize the rich interdependence between biological species which sustains life on earth.

Animals at Home, by Saraswati Dalal. Bird and insect homes display a variety of architectural forms. This book describes some of these intricate constructions and the kind of cooperation among individuals that is required in its maintenance. The emphasis will be on native species whose homes are visible and familiar to students in their daily experience.

History and Social Studies

Prehistory and Anthropology for Indian Schools, by Radhika Herzberger. A collection of materials designed for Middle and High School students, this text traces paths the human race has travelled from its African origins through the Stone Ages to the beginnings of settled life, with detailed case studies of tribal cultures in India that have survived into the 20th century. Introduces basic concepts such as culture and its relations to technology and geography, following the central theme that human beings are part of nature and depend upon the earth's varied resources for survival. Materials are presented and organized with a view toward reducing students alienation across caste, social status and economic class lines.

Ancient History for Indian Schools, by Radhika Herzberger. A political and cultural history of ancient India for High School. Introduces historical method and the contributions of archeology, linguistics and art history to our understanding of the past. The tesxt distinguishes myth from history while using both to bring the material to life. Historical facts are embedded in meaningful human contexts through semi-fictional reconstructions of life in remote times.

A History of Rishi Valley School, by Dr. Roshan Dalal. A study of the origins, growth and educational development of Rishi Valley as an English-medium residential school, and its evolution into a Resource Centre encompassing rural education, teacher training, Telugu-medium satellite schools, local crafts development, reforestation and environmental programmes.

Children in the Middle Years, by Alok Mathur. A developmental study of students growing up with their peers in a boarding school during the transition between junior and senior school.

Mathematics Programme

Pattern Language, by P.K. Srinivasan. A noval approach by a distinguished educationist, which introduces algebra through the two basic notions of constancy and change in visible patterns, and so conveys abstract notions in concrete ways accessible to children as young as eight years of age. Equally well suited for rural and urban students.

Enrichment Materials for Mathematics, by Dr. Shailesh Shirili. A set of booklets in various fields of mathemetics based on the author's rich experience in setting problems and organizing training courses for the International Mathematics Olympiads.

Oral Traditions Project

Language Through Legends. A set of graded Telugu Readers and Work Books based on local lore, in the local idiom. Jointly produced by staff Rishivanam and Rishi Valley Schools. Suitable for Schools and adult literacy programmes (Telugu).

Women at Work, by Afeefa Banu. This project will record the local oral traditions of women working in sustainable agriculture, and the rituals of fertility and harvest that are helping to preserve native varieties of grain seeds at a time when their existence is threatened on global basis.

Songs, Stories and Theatre Kits

Vennala Vindu ("A Moonlit Feast"), by Jai Sitaram Poems and songs for children, with artwork by the noted illustrator T. Gangadhar (Telugu). Published by Graphics Den, Hyderabad.

The Panchatantra in Song, composed by Vejendla Sambhasivarao. Includes a manual on shadow puppetry, an audio cassette, and a paper puppetry kit adapted from the toru bomlatta style of leather puppets from nearby Nimmalakunta in Andhra Pradesh (Telugu).

Tales From the Puranas, by Vatsala Parchure. Mythological stories retold for students for the elementary school. The kit will include a manual on puppetry together with a dramatized version of these stories on audio cassette (Hindi).

18

MAHATMA MANGAT RAM AND SANGAT SAMATAVAD

—LATE D.N. SARAF

Mahatma Mangat Ram Ji

India is, and has been a land of seers from the beginning of history. Shri Satguru Mangat Ram Ji stands in this great tradition connecting the past with our present, and with the future of mankind.

His life was one of continuous meditation, his penance refined and selfless beyond belief.

Whenever in the world the Divine manifests, it touches the receptive. We are enabled to see deeper than fractionalism and disharmony, into the nature of being itself, whole and entire. This invariably inspires, generating serenity, and strengthening the will.

The God-inspired verses and prose sayings of Shri Satguru Mangat Ram Ji admit us to the nature of being itself.

The Life of the Satguru—Briefly

— He was one of the greatest living saints of the 20th century (1903-54). He was one of the simplest and humblest. He was one of the most profound exponents of Samata: the "Sameness" between God and the world. His teachings are its guintessence. He taught nothing that he did not practise, and practise to perfection.

— A simple "five-fold path" to spiritual progress, as laid down by Satguru:

1. *Sadagi*: Simplicity—in dress, in food, in thoughts.

It is the very foundation of true and righteous life.

2. *Seva*: Service to all beings, particularly the needy - It is the principle that sustains the world. It is the supreme path that leads man to salvation.
3. *Satya*: Truth—It is Truth which abides forever. Intellect will become pure only when mind is directed towards and fixed on Truth.
4. *Satsang*: Companionship in Truth with the True-minded—It is through Satsang that one is able to discriminate between which *is* and which *is not*, and to cognise what is good and what is evil.
5. *Satsimran*: Meditation on the "Word", The Absolute—It is basic (to realisation of Truth); all other principles are supporting aids. Remembrance of the ever-existent (God) sanctifies human existence.

— On November 24th, 1903 a son was born to a pious family at village Gangothian, District Rawalpindi (now Pakistan). He was an unusual child, he seemed far too serious for his age. Mangat's father died when the child was still a four-year old infant. It was a turning point. From there on, his mother Ganeshidevi watched over him alone, and rather anxiously. Mangat preferred to stay alert in meditative stance well into midnight rather than to sleep. Returning home late from school he preferred to spend the time en-route praying in solitude, usually in a dark forest on the outskirts of the village. Only very slowly did it dawn on his infancy. Aged 13, he observed the *Chalisa*. At the climax of the 40 days' meditative fast, he experienced self-realisation.

— It was the major turning point of his life. The revelation of the Mahamantra was followed by his lifelong observance of it.

महामन्त्र

ओउम् ब्रहम सत्यम् निरंकार अजन्मा
अद्वैत पुरूषा सर्व व्यापक
कल्याण मूरत परमेश्वराय नमस्तं

(Om Brahma Satyam nirankar ajanma advait purusha sarabvyapka kalyan murat paramesvaraya namastam)

Om Brahma, Final Truth
Beyond birth
Single and undivided
All pervasive
Blessing incarnate
To You, Supreme Lord, I offer my obeisance.

— It is to be remembered that at 13 one is still a school boy.
— Mangat was exceptionally brilliant. So much so, that his headmaster, when he continued to top the list, personally offered him scholarship assistance not only upto School leaving but through undergraduate and postgraduate study as well.
— Mangat, however, consciously renounced a formal education at this point in his life. It seemed to him too self-interested. As he said of himself later: "This one's concern was with the knowledge that alone could benefit the ignorant of the world."
— Even so, his widowed mother and the family-elders prevailed upon the young boy in the hope that he would contribute to the needy household. Dutifully, if somewhat reluctantly, he undertook clerical service in Peshawar city for a while. He soon withdrew from this to set up handlooms. But that too lasted for a short time.
— Eventually he settled into a charitable practice of indigenous medicine. His spiritual preoccupation came to flower in a genuine sense of service. He charged no fees. Contributions were voluntary. His healing power acquired him a considerable local reputation. And the contributions that flowed in were set aside to feed the poor and provide them with medicaments, therapautic assistance and spiritual sustenance.
— Annually, he would organise mass-congregations at Gangothian where people were free to gather, to be fed as a community, and to derive spiritual nourishment from his discourses. This annual tradition still continues after his death, organised by a legion of Samata Ashrama throughout

the country.

— By March, 1928, with his mother's death however, Satguru Mangat Ram Ji was at last released from his final domestic responsibilities, he led an ascetic life of intense unremitting contemplation. He was at this time still a young man of 25 years. However, from this point on, there was no looking back.

— Again, while the world slept the Satguru alone sat poised and awake, in that transcendental state where Truth and Peace abide. The high mountains, deep forests, lonely spots and the open sky remained his night companions for life. A wandering faqir with no possessions but a love of God, his living was startling simple. For years at a stretch he sustained himself on a single glass of milk-tea a day. He overcame sleep, hunger and thirst.

— The greatest miracle, the Satguru always said, was life itself, and he urged the realisation of the life-force as the purpose of life. It was this very life-force that flared in him. On one occasion he fell off a sheer precipice into a deep gorge, unharmed. On another, he rested his leg into a burning tandoor but withdrew it unburned.

— His meditation itself withheld the hands of the envious and even those with murderous intent. And so he accomplished what he was sent into the world to accomplish.

— The revelatory verses of the vani welled up from the depth of his samadhi and spilled over for hours on end. Bhagat Banarsi Das who served at the Master's feet for 15 years collected as many of these he could and compiled them into Granth Shri Samata Prakash.

— The prose sayings on questions of applied Dharma and the way to right living are conserved in the Granth Shri Samata Vilas. Revelation and doctrine converge on a single focus: Samata the point where differences and duality drop.

— The sensitive reader of these two great books will himself register the pure cognitive awareness of the consciousness, indivisible from universal consciousness from which all springs.

— The Satguru's life was centred on this. "This", he said, reflecting on the oneness of the soul with God, "knows not which is the guru and which the disciple. All of us are of the nature of the divine.... The guru of this one is God Himself."

— *Samata*: Oneness, single and undivided. A state where finite melts into infinite. This was the accomplishment of the Satguru. And the way to it lies in his example: an exquisite humility, fearless and undesiring. A reverence for oneness that underlies all the apparent clutter of the many. This, and selflessness: wherever anguish, distress and poverty are to be found. Wherever being thunders into its ultimate. Beyond space. Beyond time.

His Teachings

As the greatest exponent of Samata in recent times, Satguru Mangat Ram Ji has described it copiously in his two Granths—Samata Prakash and Samata Vilas. They are like ocean of knowledge. I have selected a few pearls from this ocean. It is hoped they would be of value for all seekers, as indeed they are a source of inspiration and guidance for me.

(i) *Samata*—Sameness, oneness, non-duality, refers to a state of peace, fullness, perfection and abiding happiness.... Samata alone is bliss and every creature within is desirous of this state.... The light of oneness shines in each and every being, but due to the ego-centred mind it remains hidden.
The knowledge of oneness is achieved only on giving up the pride of the body as well as of action, that is of faith in God, God-realisation and absorption in God.... Samata-gnosis is the underlying light of all religions. It is not the creed of a denomination or of a particular religion. The real adoration of Samata-gnosis consists in perceiving God as all-pervading.... worshipping Him only and serving His creation taking it as His will.

(ii) *Soul and Body*—The dweller and the abode—The relationship between soul and body is like that of the owner and the house. The body is the house and the soul the owner of the house (body).... The self is verily different from the body; the body gets born, decays and dies; the self abides unchanging forever.
Worship the Lord—the giver of supreme blessedness, and

propitiate Him in your own house (within your mortal frame)... Through effort, man realises his Self—the True Eternal Element and sees the body as a fleeting entity. Then he sings, with supreme love, the glory of the Lord—his Self, and himself lives in self-forgetful humility. His own human self appears a mere non-entity to him for he sees all power as from the Lord.

(iii) *Shabad Brahma*—the word-and its resonance—The word is life, the Word is the life-force.... The Eternal Word has neither a beginning nor an end; it is present in all, yet it is uninvolved.... It is through right endeavour alone tht the Transcendent Word (Atman) can be experienced.

'Each pore and part of your being will resound with the eternal Word which liberates. You will hear the tune of the unstruck sound (Anahad Nad), when incoming and outgoing breath are integrated.... When the word peals within, the mind gets lost in Void.... In that abode of one's own being bliss supreme resides.'

(iv) *The Mission of Life*—The right objective of life is to be free from bondage.... Goal of human life is to realise the fearless state of peace, that is a state of joy which is not subject to variation.

The (true) purpose of human life is that the embodied soul is able to achieve its real abode of Samata Anand (unison with the Supreme Being).

(v) *Malady of Desire*—It is desire, in the form of ignorance, which tethers individual to the wheel of becoming.... There is no end to this mysterious cycle of the world of desires... Keeping desires under control is verify the greatest worship and allowing free vent to desires to control us is greatest of follies.

(vi) *Ego Obsession*—The body ego is an exceedingly subtle and deceptive force.... The real cause of human being's restlessness is ego or the feeling that 'I am the doer'.... The knowledge of imperishable and the uninvolved Reality within gives freedom from the feeling of doership.

As long as the intellect is in the grip of ego, it is a prisoner of innumerable desires and due to frightful play of mind and senss it is ever restless. This is a stat of utmost suffering.... Every effort should be made to get rid of the impurity of ego, that is, doership. Liberation from ego is a great blessing and major goal of life.

(vii) *True Faith*—True faith alone is real life.... Devoid of true faith one can achieve neither worldly progress nor spiritual merit. The person who has full faith in God, whose mind is ever intent on righteousness, who ever wishes well of all, whom adversity depresses not nor pleasures puff up and who ever lives as providence would decree, that meritorious person alone knows what real Dharma (righteousness) is.

(viii) *Righteousness*—Let man ever remain steadfast on the path of righteousness.... Righteous sentiments purify the mind and enable the intellect to realise the real nature of Being. Good conduct is the first step towards the attainment of Samata.... Give up your growing greed; adopt moderation and contentment in life.... Disregarding the defects in others one should do good to them with firmness in one's own nobility.... It is the highest duty of every man to cultivate nature of non-violence (ahimsa). A life that is characterised by ahimsa is truly holy and beneficent.

(ix) *Death*—A perfect Teacher—One who forgets death is a guideless atheist, and assuming life as unending, commits many wrongs... Death alone is perfect teacher; one who bears in mind that (one day) death will befall him, will avoid harming others.

A perfect person is one who remembers one's end and being thus convinced of the falsity (fleety nature) of life, serves others.... 'Remember three things: death, God and doing good to others. This will lead to fulfilment of your prayers.'

(x) *Peace*—Individual and Universal—Peace of mind is achieved when the intellect is liberated from the lurement of objects and focused on meditation on the Self... In the heart of hearts every individual desires peace without fear. There is, however, unrest because of incorrect effort towards peace.

Man may succeed in bringing under control the elemental forces of nature—the sun, the moon, the air or the water etc. but that will not relieve him from inner anxiety and restlessness.... Let man investigate into life-force, for peace within and peace without.

One can achieve peace and bliss by cultivating good

character, that is by restraining passions of desire, anger, greed, attachment, ego, etc.

Materialism or extreme attachment to the pleasures of the body leads to destruction. When common people become blinded by addiction to sense pleasures, then the very intensity of their expanding desires gives rise to disturbances and violance, which eventually prove suicidal. This is end result of unbridled hedonistic extravagance and indulgence.

(xi) *Basic similarity in the Teachings of Saints*—Founders of all religions the world over had only one aim—to redeem man from the transient world he is born in, and enable him to realise the bliss that is true and real.... It is primary duty of everybody to seek Truth. The greatness of prophets and saints alone will not bring salvation unless their noble principles are actually adopted in life.

Listen to the spiritual teachings as the essence of all saints and seers. They all suggest worship of one True Element, though the methods are diverse.... Those who realised Truth and merged into it had only one message to deliver (to mortal man) that he see, in this very frame of flesh, the Lord of the entire Universe. Every religion points out to the path of liberation-certain principles that would enable man earn it. But the foolish would not care for the path; they prefer wasting life-time on disputations concerning the path to salvation; ultimately they leave this world in great disappointment.

The philosophy of Samata is like a thread of the rosary of all religions—Hindus and others.

On the Path of Samata

1. Comfort those who are weary and heavy laden through your self-sacrifice.
2. Respect those who are least through your self-abnegation.
3. Authentic love of others is borne out of pain.
4. Nobility of character means to be available for the redress of others. Goodness looks not at the defects of others; it only does that which is good for others.
5. A wise man always behaves with the ignorant with compassion and kindness.

6. Think that others are better than yourself. Incarnate within yourself only that which is virtuous in them.
7. Be stable and constant in your behaviour. Compete not with your enemies; rather be compassionate and kind to them. This is what constitutes the dharma for those who follow the path of Samata.

Sangat Samatavad

Sangat Samatavad was registered in September, 1954 as a society with headquarters at Jagadhari. Its objectives are:

(1) This Association was founded by Late Shri Sadgurudeo Mahatma Mangat Ramji, therefore, the object of the *Sangat Samatavad* is to promote and strengthen among its members and spread among the general public the universal spiritual knowledge contained in the teachings of the above Sadgurudeo Saint with a view to inculcate eternal values among humanity and reform the social life.

(2) To impress by all possible means the necessity of the practice of the basic principles of Truth and to have a properly balanced view towards every religion, caste, creed and sect.

(3) To inculcate amongst its members the necessity of considering it their prime duty to purify their own lives and to desire the betterment of others.

(4) To enable the people to become free from the habit of useless discussions and narrow shackles of traditions, customs or conventions of different religions and countries and invoke their firm faith in selfless, righteous and benevolent actions.

(5) Sam Bhao alone is bliss (kalyan), Sam Bhao alone is the real form of Jeev-Atma, Sam Bhao alone is the real Dharma, the path of the realisation of Sam Bhao is the benevolent righteous path (Gurumukh Marg) leading to Eternity. Therefore, it shall be the duty of the Association to spread the principles of Samata and thus lead the masses towards Eternal Peace.

The fundamental principle of Samata is to believe that the body and things perceived through its sense are all mortal and the all sustaining life-force which supports the body and whole Universe into a living entity is the only Reality-Absolute. Therefore, the main object of the Sangat Samatavad is to have firm faith in the above and for the realisation of this eternal truth to remain true in thought, word and deed to the Five Basic Principles of Samata—Simplicity (Sadagi), Service (Seva), Truth (Satya), Spiritual Congregation (Satsang) and Meditation (Satsimran).

(6) To spread the principles of Samata as laid down by Late Shri Sadgurudeo Mahatma Mangat Ramji Maharaj in different parts of the world and for this purpose to open branches of the Association in other countries and to send missionaries (Bhikhsus) if and when deemed necessary.

(7) To publish literature; books and tracts and to bring out (daily, weekly, fortnightly, monthly, half-yearly or annually) magazines and periodicals as deemed necessary, in order to propagate and spread the objects of *Sangat Samatavad*.

(8) To acquire property by all lawful means for the fulfilment of the aim and objects for the Association.

The membership of the Sangat is open to every adult seeker of Truth, Righteousness and Peace of mind, of any religion, country, caste or creed, but of sound mind, who has faith in the principles of Samata as enunciated by Mahatma Mangat Ram.

The management of the Sangat is in the hands of a Board of Trustees comprising of 7 members. There is also a Central Prabandhak Mandal (CPM) comprising of 21 members. Several Samatavad Satsang venues are now operating.

The purpose of these Ashrams is that people get together and develop mutual understanding and love for their spiritual upliftment as well as service to the society. At these congregations—which are held regularly every week with monthly meetings being attended by many more persons and there is big participation in Annual Sammelans—teachings of Mahatma Mangat Ram are briefly touched upon in the beginning of this article are explained and discussed, besides teachings of many other great saints and sages of all religions. It may be noted that Samata is not restricted to any particular religion, faith, cult or belief. It is a platform open for all, an umbrella which covers the basic teachings and fundamental truth of all religions and philosophies.

It was expected that retired persons particularly when they are free from their wordly responsibilities should find time and stay at these centres for meditation and service. This part of the programme, unfortunately, has not been fulfilled as very few persons have actually relieved themselves to stay more or less permanently at the Ashrams. However, there are arrangements for the people to come and stay. For this, basic facilities have been provided at many places and people do go and stay there for short time.

19

MAHATMA GANDHI AND HUMAN NATURE

—SRIMATI KAMALA

We have so many ways to honour and to look into the life of Mahatma Gandhi: as philosopher and humanitarian, father of his country and statesman, writer and publisher, educationist and founder of a university which still flourishes in India today. Political scientists study his tenets of *Satyagraha*. Economists from the United Nations and the World Bank study Gandhi's ideas for third world development, and nutritionists examine his views on diet and health. Just visit our library in the Gandhi Centre, and explore there for yourself the almost endless facets of Gandhi's rich mind and total self-dedication which he gave the people of India and our world.

Despite all those practical contributions and concerns of Mahatma Gandhi he was, no doubt, one of the holiest men of history, living among us in our own century: a saint recognized even during his lifetime as a Mahatma, and revered in modern times as legendary saints have been. Without distorting, certainly without defying or glorifying Gandhi's character, he did indeed fulfill the criteria of saintliness that are universal to spiritual traditions and history: his purity of heart, simplicity of spirit, humility and utter compassion; his practices of prayer and fasting; his asceticism and discipline; his identification with "the poorest", the lowliest and the lost"; his serene acceptance of condemnation, and willingness to perserver in his great and selfless cause amidst the constant threat of death.

Above all he will be honoured for that great and selfless cause: Into a world given over to the destructive use of physical force as the ultimate means to the accomplishment of every end, Gandhi brought

Director, Gandhi Memorial Centre, Washington DC. 20016.

a different force, a spiritual force: soul-force he called it. How encouraging it is—I should say how blessed and exalting it is—to think that today, university classes of history, philosophy and political science study the principles and methods of *satyagraha* and *ahimsa* as they were proven to be practical and successful by a nation of four hundred million people! (I say blessed and exalting because true examination of Gandhi's ideas means studying the powers of the spirit.)

Of course, the precedence to Gandhi's message were many: Christ who taught to "love thine enemy;" and Buddha, six hundred years before Christ, who taught that "Ahimsa, harmony and non-injury is the highest law of all life."

Many others had established the principle of non-violence and love as the highest way of personal life. But Gandhi's contribution was unique in this way: The personal philosophy—i.e., for the individual-became the *premise* for an entire nation, and more, it became the promise of entire civilization. As Gandhi and India showed, a whole people can reform and transform themselves and others.

Almost from the beginning of his public life in India' Gandhi insised on identifying his life with the life of the whole people, the great masses of India. (Here we begin to get at the key to the man.) As you know, he was not the first champion of Indian independence. There were others before him: Tilak, Gokhale and Ram Mohan Roy, to name a few. But they were men separate from the masses—educated in Europe or wearing Western clothes, or speaking among the educated in English.

Then came Gandhi, and a vast gulf was bridged. He identified with the common people just as they were. This was the reason for his own adopting wearing the loincloth. For years people in the Western world wondered at his strange appearance, thinking him a little odd. But like all else he did, Gandhi even dressed deliberately: If the multitudes had little to wear, he also would wear little and share their plight.

As a little girl watching newsreels in my small hometown in Oklahoma that image seemed mysterious and wonderful to me. I intuitively understood that the man I watched walking and speaking amidst thousands of admiring people was compassionate and cheerful, yet resolute and powerful.... long before I heard of *satyagraha* or *ahimsa*. Gandhi himself was unforgetable, magnetic.

Symbolic and powerful as it was, we should only take Gandhi's simplicity on behalf of the Indian masses as an expression of the deep conviction that motivated him above all else: his faith in human nature.

It is perhaps odd that we have not addressed this point directly at any previous occasion for it is at the core of understanding *ahimsa* and *satyagraha*, and it gets to the heart of all Mahatma Gandhi ever wrote or said.

Human nature: What is man? Is he essentially a sinner? Is he hopelessly condemned to imperfections within himself and the struggle with evil in this world? Is he by nature weak or helpless against unrighteousness? Let's be frank: Millions of people in the world believe thus.

Without a doubt, Gandhi idealized human nature. From his childhood he was accustomed to stories of heroic sacrifice, of righteous forces confronting unrighteous ones and overcoming all obstacles. The divine potential of man, the central idea of the vast Indian religious lore, was part of Mahatma Gandhi's psyche.

The foundation to that thought is essentially simple, but radical: that every human soul is an emanation from God; of the same spiritual substance, and therefore capable of harmony with every other soul. Gandhi's faith was that human nature is *good*—whether actually or potentially. Think about it: The spiritual basis for that conviction also implies that the means utilized to awaken the dormant spirituality in others must be spiritual.

Gandhi's deeply held spiritual beliefs on human nature were not exclusively Hindu, a fact which he himself was eager to explain. He often acknowledge his debt to Christ's Sermon on the Mount, to the writings of Tolstoy and Thoreau, and the teachings of Zoroaster, Mohammed and Buddha, in addition to his beloved *Gita* and *Upanishadas*.

And so, one could be of any religious persuation and practice *satyagraha*, but the assumptions on which it rested were (and are) spiritual: The soul alone lives. Therefore, it is worthwhile fighting and even dying for causes which transcend one's selfish or personal interests. Ignite that "divine spark" in man, and let him arise to his hidden nobility. No oppressor can crush the imperishable, indomitable soul of man.

The appeal was high and strong, and it was more than mere platform moralizing. Imagine having such faith in oneself in the face of violent danger, believing that the soul's power of peace is greater than brute force. Imagine the conviction that duty to the soul is greater than duty to an unjust law, even if it is a law of one's own country. And my friends, imagine the change possible to our world by such belief!

Gandhi taught that to *feel* free is to *be* free; to stand erect like men and live in proud and equal dignity is to cast off the chains from one's spirit. That must come first, even if social freedoms are slower to realize, because once one realizes his inner freedom, no one can continue to keep him under subjugation. Why fear the foe without? As Gandhi would explain, only those fear who are so weak within that they collapse at the least show of force. And it is the weakness in us that resorts to brute force.

Indian people proudly hail the Mahatma as the father of their country. They rightly credit him for unifying, lifting and guiding them to freedom. Gandhi wanted India to be free, of course, but his standard was not nationalism. It was civilization. Put another way, it was the realization of the *civilizing force* of humanity: the power of spirit, or its *nature*—peaceful and loving.

I wonder how many people in our world are ready to exercise that *civilizing force* of human nature: to choose the courageous force of love instead of cowardly brute force? to value spiritual progress more than material gain? above all, to recognize the sanctity of the truthful means of achieving anything, especially peace.

Such unquestionable faith in mankind and unshakable optimism were often criticised—not only Gandhi's faith and optimism, but Buddha's and Christ's, and Socrates', and Chaittanya's—to name a few who set forth the same standard of civilization.

And sometimes we too wonder whether it is possible for mankind ever to be at peace with one another. The very question was put to Gandhiji in an interview. His response was characteristically simple—perhaps even self-evident.

He answered this way: The world will be at peace only when the individuals comprising it make up their minds to do so. None can deny the possibility nor say that it cannot come to pass. Such questions are an idle waste of time. *To a good man, the whole world is good.* By following this golden rule (one) can live in peace under all circumstances, believing that what is possible for him to be is also possible for others.

20

MAHATMA GANDHI'S HOLISTIC VISION OF LIFE

—SRIMATI KAMALA

Today we give our homage to Gandhi in a most sublime way-by seeing him as an Advaitist-as one totally committed to belief in the absolute oneness of all that lives. This may sound abstract or impractical at first, but it is not, and it is the very essence of all that Gandhi thought and lived.

Let me first draw to mind three critical issues of vital, practical concern to every one of us today. Then let us see how only by this very comprehensive or holistic philosophy of Gandhiji's can we find a way to face them with understanding and wisdom.

First, Nature: Undisturbed, Nature maintains a relative balance of cooperative and competitive existence. Yet, by man's predatory imposition on Nature, one-third of the earth's land is already desert; the rest is eroding unceasingly. Greed or shortsightedness compels acceleration of agricultural production by means which yield food that is organically unwholesome to the consumer and to the land. Industrialized waste pollutes air and wateways and wreaks havoc on all societies.

Second, our Societies: We would all agree to the abolition of absolute poverty, hunger and want. But does that mean modernization and the triumph of Western materialism?

The third point I'm going to develop more fully. What about our values and sense of justice? The very term "developing countries" indicates worldwide confusion over basic human values of work. What constitutes "development"? To live is to grow, but towards what goal? Certainly in the West we also seek to develop, but does our development require mass production, factories and urban sprawl; large-scale chemical agriculture; drug and surgery-based health care; endless pursuit of consumer-oriented growth.

Now let us examine the wisdom of Mahatma Gandhi. Gandhi called himself a follower of the ancient ideal of "sanathan dharma". "Sanathan" identifies reality as Eternal and Omnipresent. "Dharma" is its cosmic unfoldment as Principle or Law.

Gandhi said: "There is an orderliness in the universe; there is an unalterable law governing everything and every being that exists or lives. It is no blind law, for no blind law can govern the conduct of living beings."

For Gandhi, man's effort and responsibility to find his place in the harmonious and perfect cosmic plan constitute, his destiny or his religion, called by whatever name. He often cited his most favorite scripture, the Isha Upanishad, which instructs that, indeed, heaven itself can only be attained by reconciling life in this finite world with the infinite. In that we realize our oneness with all that live.

> "By wise utilization of the objects of the finite world one gains freedom of mind, and by the right realization of the Infinite he attains the liberation of the Self."

These concepts are the foundation of the practice of ahimsa (non-violence) and satyagraha (adherance to Truth): basically, a reverence for the indwelling life of all.

Gandhi was surrounded by religious lore and experience which awakened in him deep reverence for the non-violent life. I recall a story from the life of Buddha that must have been known to Gandhiji: It describes Buddha as a young renunciate in a forest happening upon a beautiful bird that had just been wounded by a hunter's arrow and lies suffering to death. Buddha prays lovingly and heals the young animal, but the eager hunter breaks into the tender scene to retrieve his prey. "Give him to me. He's mine. I killed him," demands the hunter.

"He's mine", responds the Buddha, "for I gave him life."

Gandhi felt that the more helpless a creature, the more entitled it is to protection by man-especially from the cruelty of man.

Gandhi revered Nature and he prayed for its indwelling spirit to purify and to heal him-physical, mentally and spiritually. He said:

> "Far more indispensable than food for the physical body is

> (this) nourishment for the soul. One can do without food for a considerable time, but a man of the spirit cannot exist for a single second without spiritual nourishment."
>
> "Just as this physical purification is necessary for the health of the body, even so spiritual purification is necessary for the health of the soul."

I have shared the soul-stirring devotions at dawn along the Ganges River at Varanasi in India, when thousands of devout people bow to the Dawn, addressing the processes and powers of creation as kin. Usha, the Dawn, lifts her gaze over the horizon and illumines the world of man with her embrace of living light. Devotees enter the river to bathe with the prayer that the holy stream of life may purify and bless them with the realization that the same divine power links life within and without. The ritual is as old as the Vedic Age, whose truth was proclaimed in the *Mandukya Upanishad*: "The soul of man is of identical nature with the God of the universe."

Gandhi's ideas about health were not based on vanity or attachment to life in the physical body, but, once again, on the natural order of the world. The body is a gift from God, a temporary garment or possession of the Soul, for the service of self-unfoldment. As embodied spirits our well-being is related to the life around us. Gandhi was convinced that disease can be prevented (or cured) if one lives more consciously in harmony with nature's forces.

Whenever he could Gandhi slept under the open skies, and he purposely held his prayer meetings on open ground where all devotees meet God together in the sacred cathedral of Nature—where there are no separations of religious distinction, no artificial barriers to the spirit.

I think he was the first in India to promote what we in America call "health food stores", the Khadi Gramodyog Bhavans where whole, unprocessed foods are available. He wore only "ahimsa" leather sandals from cows that had died a natural death, and he promoted fabrication of only "ahimsa" silk from cocoons whose worms were allowed to mature to fly away instead of being killed.

Wisely, Gandhi discerned what I would call a moral appropriateness of our conduct with nature:

> "Contrary to the Hindu precept of non-killing (he said).... I felt it was quite moral to kill serpents, bugs and the like.... But one thing took deep root in me—the conviction that morality is the basis of things and that truth is the substance of all morality."

Gandhi's practical ideas about work and economics derive clearly from his deep reverence for the unity of life. He would ask us: Does your work respect the essential symbiosis of life? Does it give hope for a better life? Does it remove difficulties and suffering? Does it raise your moral and spiritual consciousness?

Our work has a three-fold spiritual purpose or value: First, it joins us to the universe of unfolding life (nature and society); hence, it is a service. Second, it draws forth the creative potential of the human soul; hence, it is constructive and progressive. Third, when it is performed without attachment (i.e., greed, desire for recognition, pleasure or rewards) it is self-liberating.

> "O Bharata, the ignorant ones, desirous of personal good, perform actions with sensory attachment. But the wise work with an impersonal attitude and spiritual vision for the good of all beings."
>
> (*Srimad-Bhagavad Gita III*, 25)

Gandhi observed that Nature in its economic wisdom instinctivly fulfills the primary needs of hunger, shelter, procreation and growth. The continuous "Work" of Nature is a perfect socio-economic system: It is predictable, cooperative and organized. Its wages are honest, and its participants serve a common cause, though unconsciously.

We humans by definition utilize the additional dimension of free will, with a consciousness that is both creative and introspective. This God-given distinction makes us the moral costodians for the welfare of nature as well as our human society. Our trouble as humans in this natural work force is twofold: We're free to choose or assign work, and we determine the wages for our efforts.

Typically he looked to the Cosmic Whole for the standard of human conduct, saying that everything has come from God and belongs to God. Therefore, all things must be for all God's people—as a whole.

Poverty was never Gandhi's standard of spirituality. Riches do not harm per se, but as a form of power they may be used in a beneficial or harmful way. When an individual earns more than his proportional needs he should feel that he is a trustee of that surplus portion for God's people and for God's purpose.

He wanted the rich to employ wealth in service of society. He was never for expropriating or liquidating the rich; he wanted them to utilize their skills and talents voluntarily in honest and fruitful ways for the country.

Thus, for Gandhi there should be no feud between the personal and social aims and spiritual goals. Only those pursuits unrelated to the spiritual whole are unrighteous. For instance, living in total pursuit of the evanescent glories of the world is unwholesome. As wordly wealth itself is impermanent, to pursue prosperity alone is to disengage life from the Eternal.

What Gandhiji brought to life was interdisciplinary—a symbiotic, wholistic approach—a spiritual GNP—a unity of God-Nature-Person. He urged us to be spiritual-respecting the cosmic unfoldment of life. And he urged us to be rational, to "work" with Nature, the material alma mater of life; to value its irreplaceable resources; to discontinue privileges and subsidies in the economy because this is contrary to the natural law.

Almost a century ago, he urged us to use only "positive" technology—the sun, water and earth—as much as possible instead of continually thoughtlessly squandering our non-renewable resources. His ancient wisdom was truly visionary, for such sensible and obvious suggestions were based on a reverence for the oneness of life and the human aspiration for higher human consciousness of that spiritual reality.

PART III

AN ACTION PLAN

21

VALUE EDUCATION IN KENDRIYA VIDYALAYA SANGATHAN

—MULK RAJ CHILANA

Introduction

Keeping in view the importance given by the Government of India to inculcate values through school education, the KVS took an initiative in setting up a pilot project on value education. Kendriya Vidyalaya Sangathan (KVS) has been intimately involved in the Standing Committee of Planning Commission as well as in other non-governmental organisations. The lead taken by the KVS in this regard envisages preparation of a viable programme which can be tried as pilot project before disseminating the findings to other schools under KVS or suggesting the same to Education Departments elsewhere.

The Project aims at identifying potential school programmes for value development among students. This requires identification of values, methodology of imparting values, preparation of teachers for imparting values, evolving of strategies for professional growth of teachers and looking to the directions necessary for implementing the scheme as a pilot project. As a first step, it is considered necessary that an action plan is prepared which may be further improved with the guidance of educational experts, practising teachers, experienced principals and educational administrators etc.

The proposed action plan for middle classes in KVS includes content of values in the context of school, suggested methodologies, gearing of co-curricular activities for value education, setting up of whole school atmosphere to be conducive to value education, preparation of suitable materials for teachers and students, analysis

Consultant, School of Practical Philosophy, Johannesberg, South Africa.

of existing text-books helpful in promoting values or otherwise, orientation of teachers, evaluation of values, involvement of parents and community, utilisation of mass media, coordination with different agencies at local, regional and central levels, and significant guidelines for launching the project. All these aspects are briefly discussed in this Action Plan.

Value Content

In due consideration of the implementation of Value Education Programmes by different agencies and institutions in the country, it is important for KVS to focus on such values to be imparted to students as well fit in the secular character of the Constitution and the pluralistic nature of Indian society. These values should be effective in producing useful citizens of a democratic, modern and progressive society committed to scientific attitude. Such values should be free of any regional, religious and other biases. Keeping this in consideration the values accepted for implementation of the scheme in this pilot project are classified in four areas as under:

1. Values related to the area of Communication.
2. Values related to the area of Work.
3. Values related to the area of Service.
4. Values related to the area of Citizenship.

Values related to the area of ommunication include respect for the truth, listening with interest, respect for precision, courtesy, acceptance of others' views and respect for others' feelings, courage to admit mistakes and improve upon one's one faults, reflective thinking, respect for critical analysis, respect for reasoning and scientific outlook and spirit of inquiry.

Values related to the areas of work include readiness for taking initiative, resourcefulness, hardwork, perseverance, honesty and integrity, devotion to duty, punctuality, dignity of work, joy in work, responsibility, self-confidence, team spirit, cleanliness and orderliness.

Values related to the area of service include love, compassion, concern for others, love for home and family and love for environment.

Similarly, values related to the area of citizenship include respect for democracy and egalitarianism, respect for the Constitution, public property and elders, acceptance of secularism, respect for cultural heritage and social justice.

The four areas enumerated above include almost every aspect of the development of an individual as well as social reconstruction. However teachers should not feel to be bound for limiting themselves only to the above, nor should they be under any obligation to cover all the above. Therefore, the master value is considered to be 'Righteous Conduct'. This master value leads an individual to realise the significance of love, truth, peace and non-violence which are five fundamental values accepted by almost all reports on Values Education in the Planning Commission and Ministry of HRD.

Methodology

The methodology of imparting instructions in values is very important. Care must be taken that values are not taught but evolved through active involvement of students and teachers wherever possible. Community and other organisations from local, regional and national levels will also be involved in implementation of the project.

The methodology of learning values should also consider that all subjects have the potential for imparting values. Co-curricular activities can also be geared for value learning. Total School atmosphere is to contribute to imbibe necessary values and importance must be given to provide such facilities as are required for adoption of effective methodology for imparting values to students.

It has been accepted, in principle that all subjects have the potential for communicating values and drawing from them more or less desired consequences. There could be three approaches for teaching subjects alongwith values viz.

(a) direct moral instructions,
(b) methods where teachers wait for favourable circumstances to impart values, and
(c) the integrated approach to make total school programme receptive to value education.

While teaching subjects, teachers should take due care wherever it is possible to highlight a value which is possible to bring the lesson. Sometimes teachers consider that syllabus is too heavy for them to allow any deviation to focus on the values. But it must be made clear to the teachers that learning is more important than teaching and it takes place even without teaching. Therefore, focus on values should be primary for teachers.

Evaluation

Evaluation will have three phases in this project. One, to evaluate the students to find out how far they have incorporated in their personalities the values which have been earmarked for programme, second, to evaluate the scheme to find out the success of the project and third, to evaluate how the teachers have grown in their efficiency during implementation of the project.

The impact of the project of the students will be evident from how far the students are able to appreciate the values and incorporate the same in their behaviour patterns. Thus the impact of the project will be judged not only from the understanding of values by students but also the effective domain of the project. For evaluation of this type it is necessary to have continuous and comprehensive evaluation procedures. The teachers may judge the behaviour of students in day-to-day life of the school. An anecdotal record of incidents which are conducive or otherwise may be kept or the cumulative record card of the students may indicate such happenings. It is also intended to have an evaluation tool so that each student may evaluate his or her own progress in this regard. Group evaluation may also be tried. Teachers may formulate questions for the written examinations which may reveal how far the students have learnt the values and are motivated to exhibit them in their daily behaviour. Exemplary question papers may be supplied to such schools and used for training the resource persons and through them all other teachers.

It is often felt that the scheme of value education as such also needs to be evaluated. This is necessary because the scheme is to be extended to other schools after the trial of one year as a pilot project. Some of the important aspects to be considered in this regard are to find out how far the project has been implemented in selected schools and to judge how far the students can appreciate the values as alternate course of behaviour. In order to evaluate the project as such techniques like anecdotal records, checklists, personal interviews and questionnaires may be applied.

It will be relevant to evaluate the project from another angle as to how far teachers have grown in their efficiency to reach out to the children and to appreciate the significance of the project. Thus, the project is likely to have impact on the professional efficiency of the teacher, too.

It is important to remember that while evaluating the students should not be compared with each other. Each student should be compared with his/her previous status. The teacher should also adopt a kind and positive approach in the implementation and evaluation process. The teacher should make a rapport with the child and not necessarily communicate the award to the students. But the evaluation must pave the way for better behaviour by the children.

Relevent Materials

Because of the innovative nature of the project and the systematic way in which it is expected to be implemented, some related materials may be prepared at the headquarters for the guidance of Principal, teachers as well as students. The most important write-ups in this regard is the preparation of a handbook for teachers, some supplementary reading materials for children and evaluation tools for teachers and students.

The handbook for teachers may include detailed description of the values and how they can be developed through a variety of methods including curricular and co-curricular activities of teaching and learning. It should also include selected materials of every subject and how teacher can indirectly incorporate a few values in relation to the content material in the textbooks of the students. The handbook will indicate how co-curricular activities like games, dramatics, singing, scouting, and Yoga classes can be utilised for learning teaching of values. The handbook should also mention how specific activities like talks in the morning assembly and services of experts from local, regional and national levels may be utilised for the purpose.

Attempts should be made to prepare additional reading material for the children of classes VI, VII and VIII. These materials will highlight the need for imbibing values. These materials will be developed in the form of stories, plays and kits etc.

Apart from the material for teachers and students evaluation tools will be prepared to gauge the impact of value education on students. Self-evaluation tool by the children will be used apart from other evaluation techniques.

It has also been visualised that guidelines for implementation of school-based in-service education of teachers are provided so that teachers may gain sufficient knowledge about the project. This plan is intended to help teachers to utilise their own initiative and develop themselves through reading, writing, self-evaluation and action research. The write-up will be prepared with special reference to teacher preparation for imparting value education to students.

Text-Book Analysis

Analysis of the existing text-books in all subjects for classes VI to VIII will be a continuous process. The hand-book for teachers is, in fact, based on the preliminary analysis of textual material which students utilized in their classes. The purpose of the analysis of the text-books is to find out which areas of lessons are more conducive for development of desirable values among the children. Similarly, those areas will also be identified which hinder the imbibing of desirable values by students during the process of the operation of these pilot projects. Strategies will be developed to tackle both the areas. These analysis will be ultimately useful for revision of the text-books for which suggestions will be given to the writers of the text-books in the NCERT. Another useful clue in this regard will be gained from the teachers as to how more content areas can be added so that courses may be enriched with values.

Orientation of Teachers

Orientation of teachers is the key area for the success of the programme. When selected schools will send teachers for preparation of handbook, they will indirectly be acquainted with the programme which is to be implemented in their schools. It is, therefore, decided to get three teachers from each region for preparation of the handbook. In addition to this, orientation programmes will be organised at national, regional and local levels.

At the national levels resource persons will be trained for each region. These resource persons will further organise courses at the regional level. The content of training for these resource persons will include the need and significance of the project, rationale for selecting the values, methodology of instructions of values, evaluation of values and involvement of different agencies and institutions for implementation of the project. They will also be given opportunities to discuss guidelines for launching the project. The training of resource persons will have discussions on methodology rather than lectures by experts. The resource persons will critically examine the different aspects and implement the same while training teachers at regional level.

At the regional level all teachers dealing with classes VI to VII will be oriented by the trained resource persons. A phased programme in this regard will be developed by the Assistant Commissioners. Regional level programme for orientation of teachers will be held at least twice during the operation of the pilot project. The second programme of orientation will provide opportunities to the teachers to discuss their doubts and gain more clarity in develoing the programme.

Teacher development programmes at the school level will be very useful. Therefore, school-based in-service education will be stressed. Guidelines for working out the procedures will be prepared. The schools may provide opportunities in the staff meetings to discuss the programme of value education specially keeping in view its difficulties. Some local experts may also be invited to speak to teachers in each school. School-based in-service education will be an opportunity for continuous development of the teachers, for this reading material may be sent from the headquarters to the schools. Teachers may also attempt to write their own experience and this will help in their professional growth. Likewise, some action research projects may be developed by each school depanding upon their needs.

Apart from the training courses from teachers as mentioned above, orientation of the Principles in two phases has been envisaged by the KVS. Similarly, all the ACs have contributed in the form of giving their reactions for implementation of the project. This has been done during the Assistant Commissioners conference.

Parental Involvement

A family constituted by the parents and children is undoubtedly the main source where early 'Sanskara' are formed. This way, children informally practise basic values like love, honesty, truthfulness, respect for elders, tolerance, punctuality, personal gladness etc. It is, therefore, necessary for a school to find out the values a child has received in the family. The school should also take into confidence the parents regarding the value pattern it has planned. So, it is very important that parents are frequently involved in the project of value orientation of education. That way, they will be able to appreciate the identified values and give them due importance. They will also follow some of such values and thus set example before their children/wards. They will have right attitude to help children and the school in implementing value education programme.

The parents can be involved in the value education project in many ways. In the meetings of PTA, the programme of value education any be discussed. Classwise meetings of the parents may also be held where suggestions of the parents may be considered for implementing the proejct. At least three meeting must be held in the year 1994-95.

Parents may also be invited in some important functioners of the KVS like Annual Day Celebration, various exhibitions, Sports Day so that they may see how value education is being imparted to the children. Parents may also be involved in improving the cleanliness of the Vidyalaya. Some of them be invited to speak on involvement of grandparents who have comparatively more time and their experience of social atmosphere will be more useful. Parents and grandparents may also be involved during the House Competitions like debate, music, drawing and calligraphy etc. The themes may be selected as related to certain values mentioned in the Action Plan.

Community Participation

Apart from the parents, community members may also be involved in the project as their participation will be more selfless. Their involvement will promote inter-dependence, communal harmony, secularism, cooperation, fellow-feeling, respect for democratic values and national integration.

The involvement of community members may be sought in many ways. People interested in value education may be invited for talks in the morning assembly or on other suitable occasions. Such members of community may be invited who can present certain values through discussions, lectures and dramatization. A good example in this regard has been set by 'Nukkad Group' where they attempt to promote communal harmony, national integration and solution to certain burning problems of the society. Skilled persons from the community can help a school in taking up activities related to work experience, SUPW and other such programmes which lead to the development attitude for dignity of work. Participation of the community may also be sought during the celebration of important days such as UN Day, Human Rights' Day and Red Cross Day. Some Govt. departments may be involved for developing civic values among the students. The Deptt. of Traffic Police may help in developing in the children values for traffic rules maintenance. Deptt. of Environment can be involved in developing among children the importance of an atmosphere in their school and neighbourhood. Apart from the community going to the school, participation of children may also be encouraged in the functions organised by the community.

Coordination

It need not be emphasised that success of the project depends upon the coordination between the local institutions/agencies and the other organisations of the school as well as liaison between the school and the regional and national institutions. The school must seek coordination and cooperation from individuals, community and voluntary organisations.

In order to promote this coordination, it may be necessary to keep these institutions/organisations in touch with the plans and project. Apart from different institutions, the school children may visit other schools, libraries, zoos, museums, exhibitions etc. The students may also visit temples, mosques, gurudwaras, churches and other religious places to have a practical understanding on values. It may also be worthwhile for children to visit other schools in their area.

All the activities undertaken by individual schools need to be coordinated at the regional level by the respective ACs. The ACs may arrange meetings of the Principals and coordinators of the project. This will help in sharing the experiences and also in solving the problems faced by the schools. AC may also provide clues about the experiments undertaken by the other institutions in the region.

The project will be getting due impetus with proper development of relevant material at the national level. This responsibility can be given to Joint Commissioner (Academic) Kendriya Vidyalaya Sangathan. KVS may also have closer coordination between the premier institutions like NCERT, NIEPA, MHRD and Planning Commission. These are major national institutions which are deeply concerned with the value education programmes. Value education projects have also been undertaken at the international level by many countries. Help may be sought from international organisations like Lion's Club, Rotary Club, Red Cross and Scouting etc.

Mass Media

The project of value orientation education can be promoted with apt collaboration and coordination. With the mass media like radio, TV and newspaper, the school may get reaction from the users of the mass media. This will motivate the mass media to highlight the need for such projects and there may be suggestions from the community for undertaking suitable activities for success of the project. All India Radio as well as television offer many programmes which are directly focused on promotion of values, but it is relevant to find out that there are also some programmes which hinder in the development of desirable values. So users of the mass media will become more cautious of the utility or otherwise of such programmes for value orientation of education.

As the project develops, authorities may approach schools for more details of the programme. Use of mass media undoubtedly will be very useful in strengthening value education.

Guidelines for Launching the Project

A school may launch the programme in a formal way or in an informal way as considered suitable by the Principal, teachers and students. If formal launching of the project is desired by a Principal, he may involve any community leader to inaugurate the plan. This will pave the way for better community participation. There is also an advantage in informal initiative of the project. This way, it will be more silent work and the community will get information as the project gets a stronger base. But in any case, every school must have one coordinator who should preferably be the Vice-Principal or a Senior PGT with the knowledge of research methodology and acquainted with the procedures for developmental projects. This will help in keeping proper records for the development of the plan. It must be remembered that each school will retain its individuality in developing the plan of value education.

22

HUMAN-VALUES: A TASK FOR ALL

—M.L. DEWAN

Introduction

In the final stages of preparation of this book and in reviewing what has been written by the various contributions, a final Chapter, an "Afterward" is needed—namely, what are our suggestions for our Action Programme for "Human-Values—A Task for All" I decided to fill in this gap.

Inspirations and Quotation

I also felt "Task for all in Human-Values" is a tall order, but I should start with some inspirations, some quotes from those who have been in leading positions like Mahatma Gandhi, Swami Vivekananda, like the Quotes from *Gita, Vedas, Upanishads* and then the present day Human-Value Promoters—So I start with such Quotes.

I quote from Human-Values—A Voyage from I to we by Antonio and Sylvie Craxi who prepared an outstanding pictorial document from European Foundation for Human-Values.

(i) "The scope of education is to form the character of the pupils, that is to say to cultivate in them the infinite potentialities of a mind nourished on the real values of human life.

In our technological era in which cultural exchanges and rapid communications make more evident the interdependence of each one of us upon the other, man becomes the heir of the moral richness of the entire human

N-44, Panchshila Park, New Delhi - 110017

race, that which is represented by the human values, the common denominator of all the religious, cultural, ethical, philosophical and legal traditions of the whole world.

To cultivate in the young the values of Truth, Moral behaviour (the right action) or *Dharma*, Peace, Love and Non-violence signifies the laying of the foundations for the construction of human personality in its various aspects: physical, intellectual, emotional, psychic and spiritual.

We nourish the hope that the best and most illuminated energies of the countries will rally around this educational project in order to enable the educational process itself to become an instrument of true moral and civil progress."

(ii) One of the First Quotes is what I wrote in "Ode to Himalayas 2nd October, 1997. We make a living by what we get but we make a life by what we give". The value is to give to our society our time, effort and service, atleast equal to or hopefully more than what we get.

(iii) "Some Succeed because they are Destined to but most Succeed because they are Determined to The Value is Determination, Hard work, hard conscious work."

(iv) Mahatma Gandhi wrote long years back in *India of my Dreams,* Navjeevan Press 1947. *Rights & Duties.* Everybody talked of Right and Human Rights what about calling "The Human Rights and Duties". The fact that Rights are being asked but duties are not being performed is an evil of the society which is giving rise to corruption.

Mahatma Gandhi in his Autobiography or the story of My Experiments with Truth wrote as early as 1927. "My uniform experience has convinced me that there is no other God than Truth. And the only means of the realization of Truth is Ahimsa-Non-Violence.... To see the Universal and all prevailing spirit of truth face to face, one must be able to love the meanest of creation as oneself. Identification with everything that lives is impossible without self-purification. Self-purification must mean purification in all the walks of life. And purification being highly infectious, purification of one self-necessarily leads to the purification of one's surroundings.

(v) Swami Vivekananda brought the Indian culture's teaching of *Vedas, Upanishads* and *Gita* to the Indian awareness of the time and more to the world as a whole starting with the Parliament of Religions in 1893 in Chicago. He highlights the Human-Values at different times and I present a few of the Quotes from Swami Vivekananda:

— Nothing is gained except by sacrifice—the holiest function of our human consciousness, the noblest, donot make it unclean.
— It is much easier to do anything upon the external plane, but the greatest conqueror in the world finds himself a mere child when he tries to control his own mind.
— The greater part of the practical lesson which the Yogi gives us is in the Mind, the power of Concentration and Meditation.
— What is the difference between man and animals? "Food and sleep, procreation of the species and fear exist in common with the animals. There is one difference Man can control all these and become God, the Master".
— The path-way to Godhead is through *The Human-Values* (inserted by the Editor).
— Happiness is not the absence of the conflict but the ability to cope with it.

Quotations for Promoting Human Values

(vi) The booklet "Great Quotations" by Great Quotations Inc Selected ones are being quoted here those that relate to Human Values.

— "Those who bring sunshine to the lives of others *cannot keep it from themselves*".
— The great acts of love are done by those (example Mother Teresa) who are habitually performing small acts of kindness).
— "The first great gift we can bestow on others is a good example."
— "Nothing happens unless first a dream."
— Courtesy cost nothing yet buys things that are

priceless.

— The smallest good deed is better than the greatest intention.
— You can teach a better sermon with your life than with your lips.
— For every minute you are angry, you loose sixty seconds of Happiness.
— Of all the things you wear, your expression is most important.
— The future belongs to those who believe in the beauty of their dreams.
— Happiness is not a state to arrive at but a manner of travelling.
— God grant me the Serenity to accept the things I cannot change, the Courage to change the things I can, and the Wisdom to know the difference.
— I cannot change yerterday, I can only make the most of today, and look with hope towards tomorrow.
— People can alter their lives by altering their attitudes.
— One person with courage makes a majority.

(vii) Take time to (also from my earlier booklet *Themes of Development II*)

Take time to work,
It is the price of success.
Take time to think,
It is the source of power.
Take time to play, it is the
Secret of perpetual Youth.
Take time to be friendly,
It is the road to happiness.
Take time to love
And be loved, it is a
Privilege of the Gods.
Take time to share, life is
Too short to be selfish.
Take time to laugh,
Laughter is the Music
Of the Soul.

(viii) Quotation from *Envisioning: A Sustaining Society* by Lester Milbrath

We are what we think
All that we are arises with our thoughts
With our thoughts we make the world.

The thought manifests as the word,
The word manifests as the deed,
The deed develops into habit,
And the habit hardens into character,
So watch the thought and its ways with care,
And let it spring from love,
Born out of concern for all beings.

(ix) Here I would like to reproduce an article from Purity, "Promoting Universal Values of life as published by "Prajapita Brahma Kumaris Ishwariya Vishwa Vidyalaya (H.Q. Mount Abu), New Delhi - 110 005. To refresh ourselves, with the thought and action that there is still hope-let us make Human Values a *Task for All.*

Value Education the Key is Spiritual Power

On the eve of Teacher's Day, 1997 educationists, political leaders and students of Delhi assembled at the Talkatora Stadium to express their concern over the erosion of values in the society and to find ways to reverse this trend. While all the eminent speakers at the 'Conference on Value Education' spoke about the dire need to impart value-education in schools and homes, the students conveyed similar sentiments through lively performances of dance, songs and skits.

Dr. Harsh Vardhan, Minister for Education, Delhi, said that teachers played a very important role in building the society, the nation and an orderly world. In the 50th year of India's Independence, it is time for introspection and for taking on the challenges faced by the nation in the field of education. He called upon educationists to help in the task of cultivating values in the minds of students. Recalling the nation's great heritage of wisdom and learning, Dr. Vardhan said that teachers can again put India on the top by imparting value education. A beginning can be made in this direction by narrating the life history of great kings and spiritual personalities of India to children who are now being fed on meaningless and negative images by TV and other media.

Mr. T.B. Venkatraman, Union Minister of Surface Transport, said that education is a comprehensive process involving commitment to pursuit of knowledge, development of character and inculcation of values. Education is inseparably bound with values. He said that teachers should conduct themselves according to the highest ethics so as to set an example for their students.

However, the task of value education should not be put on the shoulders of teachers alone, said Mr. K.B. Pawar, Secretary-General. Association of Indian Universities. He said value education has to be integrated with other activities so that everybody could contribute to it. The parents and the media also have an important role to play in this process.

Rajyogini Hirdaya Mohini, Joint Chief of Brahma Kumaris, said that though the nation had achieved independence 50 years ago, we are yet to realise Gandhiji's dream of 'Ram Rajya' (a prosperous and peaceful nation.) Today, youngsters are falling prey to various addictions and they are unable to change their habits despite their good intentions. This is due to lack of spiritual power and inner strength, she said, if each one of us takes up the task of transforming ourselves, then the world will be a better place.

B.K. Asha, a senior Rajyoga teacher, said that the true purpose of education is to bring out the divinity latent in human beings. She noted that the erstwhile instruments of education—the family, school and religious institutions—were crumbling and the youth had no role models to follow, thus leading to further devaluation of values. In this light, the teacher's role extends beyond the classroom and the role of media in building a better society is also very important, she said.

Prof. Rakesh Khurana, Pro-Vice Chancellor, Indira Gandhi National Open University, reminded that educationists should provide a code of conduct for a good social and moral order. The challenge lies in combining the utilitarian role of education with value education.

An Action Programme

Coming to the outline of an Action Programmme on "Human

Values: A Task for All" before we go into the categories of citizens who have to Act, I would like to preface it with some quotations from *Kathopanishad* to remind us, the human beings, of the totality of the whole system of Universe.

(i) "A human being is one of the approximately five billion human beings on this earth and therefore, is an infinitesimal part of the human population.
(ii) The earth is an infinitesimal part of the solar system.
(iii) The solar system is an infinitesimal part of the milky way.
(iv) The milky way is an infinitesimal part of the universe. And, even this universe is ever expanding."

If we only understand the truth contained in the above statements, we would give up the false sense of 'I', the doership attitude personal, personality, importance etc. and transcend the mundane to merge in the Purusha, the Supreme.

(a) For Parents and Children

Child is father/mother of man/woman. The human values have to be incalculated from early childhood. This fact is known but we also know that you donot promote value system or any other knowledge excepting by working as a Role Model.

(b) For School, College and all Educational Institutions

The role of school teacher is crucial in any action Programme to nourish the values initially taught at home. Family is like a Banyan tree and the branches are children and roots are the Human Values. A teacher can help the students to develop a new attitude towards their daily learnings, tasks and sports, a positive approach wanting to do something good for oneself, family, society and country.

(c) For political and social leaders—written under 6.
(d) For Government bureacracy—(the same applies as 5c.).
(e) For Urban Society

India and the world is getting urbanized rather speedily. More people are living per squares kilometer and even per square meter.

Concern for others should be high on the list of human values.

(f) For Rural Society

Environment and resource conservation and living caring for nature are some of the additional values to the basic values we have talked earlier.

Project-Building Individual Character

Quoting from my own book *Agriculture and Rural Development in India: A Case Study on Dignity of Labour*. I am quoting "A special project aimed at building individual character in India". What are the theory, practices and economics of corruption which is retarding such character building, has to be understood.

(a) Generally speaking, corruption can be defined as the inappropriate use of power or influence which somebody has because of his position. This misuse can be and is usually for:

(i) immediate private gains.
(ii) political party, and
(iii) pressure of one kind or another.

(b) Corruption has some other characteristics:

(i) those involved usually try to keep it (corruption) secret, (not any more when it has become a norm),
(ii) there are usually laws in most countries against corruption. The lawmaker has decided that corruption is punishable, but often the borderline between proper and inappropriate action is not well defined, and
(iii) This borderline is often decided by custom. Custom varies from time to time and at different places.

(c) Why is the ground fertile in some places for corruption?

(i) When the public sector expands rapidly and public

authorities take charge of commercial activities, or of new regulative functions (investments, foreign exchange control, fixing of rents, prices, allotment of houses, land, etc.).

(ii) When the social machinery and existing value concepts of a society are destroyed, or when a whole nation has to suffer hardship and starvation while individual profiteers can live in abundance and luxury, it is difficult to expect that the civil servant's sense of responsibility and loyalty shall remain unaffected, especially when he is underpaid and lacks security of tenure.

"It is hard for an empty sack to stand upright". It is difficult to require honesty when the economic pre-requisites for honesty do not exist.

(d) How to fight corruption?

(i) Build individual character
(ii) Simultaneously work on the economic pre-requisites.
(iii) Promote Human Values in all possible ways. I reproduce purpose and description of the proposed Action Project.

Purpose

1. The purpose of the project is to stimulate the development of the character of all citizens of India who are responsible and not corruptible, to become the pillars of a great country, and who will each carry out with efficiency and reliability the job or task that each one undertakes.
2. In particular, recognizing that character is built in the early years of a child, like the foundation of a building; also recognizing that even though the foundation may be strong, the building can still be weak, the project will:

(a) Study, find out and establish the reasons for the deterioration of national character, including methods for regenerating the will and determination to improve it;

(b) Stimulate effective and practical measures to teach at an early age in all the schools the principles and practices of high character.

(c) To bring in the principles and practices of absence of corruption in everyday living in homes, in business, in offices, in the field, in politics, so that the growing children and future citizens do not get disillusioned by seeing that all they were taught in schools is not applicable to everyday life; and

(d) Leaders of men, in political, educational and other fields should be persons who are not corrupt nor corruptible as they are the ones who set examples to others.

Description of the Project

Specific actions such as follow will be stimulated:

1. *At Home*: Guidance of mothers and parents to bring up the children properly and adequately and assist in building their character from the beginning. At Central, State, District and Thana, or Block level, organizations of enlightened mothers, few but devoted and volunteers: their task is to show how important it is to have a strong character, to be honest, to do one's share of work, to be truthful, to do one's civic duties, even to do voluntary work for national welfare and development.
2. *In Schools*: Good, selected, well-trained moderately wellpaid teachers. The curriculum to be worked out carefully; and properly prepared text-books with practical exercises should be usd. In studies, in games, and otherwise, the emphasis should be placed on strength to stand up to injustice, nepotism, unfairness, etc. Movies, trips, camps, establishment and running of school garden plots and school forests, which are useful for practical work to gain an understanding of the importance of various relevant factors in character building, should be included where possible in school activities.
3. *In Colleges and Universities*: Every student for one out of 2-3 summer vacations, must join training and practical camps (also give one or more year of his life to the country).

If necessary, a law should make it compulsory that each youth should give one or two years to military and civil training. (Can we organize it? Yes, give 1-2 years to organize-curriculum should be worked out taking NSS, NCC as examples) and building on these experience.

4. *In Business*:

   (a) that holiday camps should be organized at the important holiday resorts, for medium to big business men for a few weeks each, where they are invited and the importance of character discussed through movies, seminars, skits, mode of living, Yoga and meditation sessions etc.
   (b) Day to day activities be monitored and methodology developed for inculcating human values and sound character in all business dealings.

5. *For Offices*: Government offices—there is to be more responsibility given to each person and there should be fewer people in every office, varying according to the need. There should be fewer steps for each task. (The project approach to actual development should be enunciated. To define the Project Approach "A Special Project Aimed at Improving National Institutions in India.") be given greater emphasis.
6. *For Political and Public Office Holders*: Complete honesty and cleanliness in their jobs and dealings.
7. *For Industrial Workers*: Holiday camps should be organized and planned. Courses be planned or videos be shown indicating the importance of hard work and sound character, which should work positively and for increased production.
8. *For Farming Population*: Offering them the leadership and incentive to work harder and increase production. The leadership should help to remove the bottlenecks or impediments for and promote their self reliance through the efficient use of land, water, crops, forests, cattle, and integrated use of such resources.

A Plea for Quality

We are fond of displaying our quantity, to show that we are a big nation, a nation of 980 million people. Our plans are big, we talk big. We have produced 180 million tons of foodgrains, we produce so many million tons of steel including steel ingots, saleable steel casting. We have built so many dams each having so many million cubic metres of water. We have started so many community development blocks. These are large and impressive numbers indeed.

We know that number or quantity is important, but we should not forget Quality. Let us produce quality children, give them good quality education, so that each one will be worth much more. In terms of good production, let us not only talk of producing rice and wheat, but let us produce more grapes, apples, vegetables, pulses, beans, milk and milk products, meat and meat products, fruits, etc. This is quality food, we are doing these but we can and need to do more of these.

We talk of 105 Universities plus so many institutes deemed to be universities, several thousands of colleges and several hundred thousand of schools. It is good to spread education, learning, knowledge. But knowledge is power only when it helps some production and furthers Right Action. To know how to grow melons is of no value unless you grow them, or teach others by growing them. Let us have practical schools for agriculture, technology, for trades and professions. Often agricultural schools and colleges have not enough or even any land where students can grow crops. Imagine, the diploma or degree which is supposed to indicate that you know how to do a particular work which becomes an end in itself and not the knowledge or experience that you get from this education.

The quality of men and material is important. We should build houses which last, roads which will not be easily washed away or dams which will not be silted up and become useless. We build dams, large canals and irrigation network without ensuring that every bit of the water stored or canalized is fully utilized. This is like buying a lot of bread when you are hungry, consuming what you need immediately and wasting the rest. This is happening with the irrigation canals and systems in many places.

Even on the food front, there is information that if only half the losses during harvesting and storage of foodgrains are eliminated, we will have enough food to both consume and export. We produce the food but we do not have it (because we waste it). We have immense store of Solar energy and we can use much more of such energy through solar devices, wind and water power (mini and micro) —also efficiently use wood resources rather than use too much of non-renewable resources like oil, coal etc.

By concentrating on the quality, the implication is that each operation has to be given adequate emphasis. It is a matter of detail that one goes into that makes for quality. A nation or people are respected much more if there is quality. We have resources and brains. Let us muster the will to produce more of good quality things. At this stage of national emergency we need more and more quality and our past achievements show that we can do it.

All the above are what I mean by Action Programme for Promoting Human Values.

An Indian Edition of "Human Values"

"A Voyage from I to We" is under preparation—based on the lines of what Prof. Antonio and Sylvie Craxi have prepared for "European Foundation for Human Values". It has aimed at Basic Human Values-applicable for all Humanity Plus Values which are the outcome of our civilization and culture and is recommended for further reading.

A commission on Human Values is essentially one to help the whole Society fight out the Evils of Corruption which is our concern for our society.

Citizenship Development Societies

Be further stimulated (in all parts of the country, about on the lines of Citizen Development Society of Delhi (1, West Kidwai Nagar, New Delhi-110 023). A consortium of C.D.S. be framed in various parts of the country and a National Seminar be held on the subject of Promotion of Citizen Development based on Value System on Quality of our citizenship and on lines of several agencies promoting value system given in Part II of this book be promoted hopefully before the end of the century.

Or Else

This leads me to "Or Else" I would quote here what I wrote from the "The Themes of Development—A Warning : Save Himalayas —*Or*

Else, January, 1989.

Himalayas must be conserved, saved and developed *Or Else*, be prepared for:

— More severe cycles of droughts and floods.
— More severe landslides and dislocation of communications.
— Severe water famines in the Himalayas—source of snow, river and spring water.
— Greater migration of Hill people to the plains with increasing slums in the cities.
— Serious scarcities of wood, fuel and fodder with consequent effect on the country as a whole.
— Never ending spiral of rising prices.
— Collapse of land use, law and order, even political, social and economic decay.
— Even the Himalayas turning into a dry, high arid desert like Afghanistan, Lahul Spiti, and Ladakh.

So the Himalayas must be saved. We must all act and execute our tasks sincerely, consciously and determinedly, NOW.

Similarly I can predict a warning: Promote and Inculcate Human Values—As a Task for All.

Or Else

— *More corruption in all sphere of Human Life.*
— Including in education where schools and colleges will be turned into business houses and money-making institutions.
— In social and economic institutions turning into money making self-seeking and corrupt organisations.
— In political field-those who are to govern will do all tasks excepting to govern.
— Multiplicity of scam, large-scale embazzlement of public funds leaving less time and money for development and welfare. Leaders quarelling among themselves less on principles but more for power, egoism and selfishness.
— Poverty to continue or worsen not only as a disease-a symbol of under development, a whirl pool of squalor and filth out of which only a few will be able to get out.

— Never ending spiral of rising prices.
— Collapse of law and order, political, socio-economic and even environment decay.

The human values, and character as nation building activities must be given *highest priority* and a *task for all.* It is possible that *Mass Media* and *Globalization* are playing, havoc with the minds of the New Generation and a cultural degeneration has set in. Ours is a blessed country and it will come out of the degradation through a new leadership. If not, God is our ultimate saviour.

The Prayers

I close this chapter by reciting a Prayer for giving us strength and courage to undertake this huge task by citizens and not by Government alone for the future of India.

May we as nation be guided by the Divine to rediscover the sacred flame of our national heritage, which so many have given their lives to safeguard;
Let the wounds of separation and division be healed by opening our hearts to listen to the truth on all sides, allowing us to find a higher truth that includes us all;
May we learn to honor and enjoy our diversity and differences as a people, even as we more deeply touch our fundamental unity;
May we, as a people, undergo a transformation that will draw forth individuals to lead our nation who embody courage, compassion and a higher vision;
May our leaders inspire us, and we so inspire each other with our potential as individuals and as a nation, that a new spirit of forgiveness, caring and honesty be born in our nation;
May we, as a united people, move with clear, directed purpose to take our place within the community of nations to help build future for all humankind.
May we as a nation rededicate ourselves to truly living as one nation, under God, individuals, with liberty and justice for all; and hold dear the basic human values like Truth, Non-violence, Right action or Dharma, Peace and Love.
And may God's will be done for India as we, the people

align with that Will.

I am annexing THE LIMA DECLARATION Sept 1997, of citizens drawn from 93 countries after a searching discussion of the MEANS TO CONTAIN CORRUPTION IN ALL ITS MANIFESTATIONS AROUND THE GLOBE. I trust this Declaration will stimulate the readers to an Action Programme for treating Human Values—as a Task for All.

ANNEXURE

THE LIMA DECLARATION

LIMA, PERU, 7-11, SEPTEMBER 1997

WE, citizens drawn from 93 countries, coming from all the continents and from countries large and small, in every stage of development, rich and poor, and from varied backgrounds in government, the private sector, and civil society.

AFTER a searching discussion of the means to contain corruption in all its manifestations around the globe and united on our vision of an era of international and national co-operation in the twenty-first century in which the evil of corruption is suppressed.

NOW JOIN TOGETHER in this Declaration of the 8th International Conference Against Corruption held in Lima, Peru from 7-11 September 1997.

CONVINCED that corruption

Erodes the moral fabric of every society; violates the social and economic rights of the poor and the vulnerable; undermines democracy; subverts the rule of law which is the basis of every civilised society; retards development; and denies societies, and particularly the poor, the benefits of free and open competition **BELIEVING** THAT:

Fighting corruption is the business of everyone throughout every society; the fight involves the defence and strengthening of the ethical values in all societies; it is essential that coalitions be formed between government, civil society and the private sector; there must be a sustained campaign against corruption within the private sector as, with greater privatisation and deregulation, it assumes a greater role in activities traditionally performed by the state; and top leadership sets the tone in all societies, as "You clean a staircase by starting at the top" **WE NOW CALL UPON** governments, international and regional agencies and citizens around the world to mobilise their efforts and energies to join us in achieving the following actions:

Actions at the International and Regional Level

International institutions must support more fully the creative role civil society has to play in advancing the development of good governance and work with them in partnership to this end. They must work together to emphasise the positive aspects of globalisation, and to contain its negative elements.

Tax deductibility of bribes by which exporting countries actively subsidise and encourage the corruption of officials in other countries must be ended.

The **OECD** should complete a convention to criminalise the bribing of foreign officials by the end of this year, and its member states should implement its provisions before the end of 1998. All states of the Americas should ratify the Inter-American Convention Against Corruption before the Summit of the Americas in Santiago in March, 1998.

The World Bank and the IMF should accelerate implementation of their new policies against corruption and particularly the suspension of lending to governments who do not adequately address the corruption issue.

The European Union should accelerate implementation of its own anti-corruption policies recommended by the Council of Ministers of the EU in May, 1997.

The World Trade Organisation (WTO) must itself join in the global struggle and begin to address the serious impact of corruption on world trade.

All multilaterial and bilateral aid agencies, together with their development partners, must find practical ways of overcomng corruption in their development programmes.

International institutions should further develop imaginative and new approaches to procurement in partnership with individual governments and the private sector, including the use of anti-bribary and integrity pacts. Bidders who bribe should be blacklisted.

International organisations with mandates in the area, including **INTERPOL** and the World Customs Organisation, should take steps to strengthen international law enforcement co-operation.

Regulation of the operations of all international banking

centres must be improved so as to ensure that assets under their control are governed by agreed international norms and that illicitly gained assets can be traced, frozen and forfeited.

The reform and modernisation of customs systems, with an emphasis on transparency and integrity, is still urgently needed in many countries.

The International Chamber of Commerce and other business organisations must promote widespread acceptance by companies of codes of conduct and compliance programmes to combat extortion and bribery at home and abroad.

The International Association of Presecutors and the International Bar Association should develop model laws whereby the prosecution of corruption cases in each of our various legal systems can be rendered less complex and more expeditious, while being consistent with international human rights norms.

Shareholders around the world should insist that the companies in which they invest subscribe to the objectives of the corporate governance movement.

The various international associations of accountants and auditors and the international associations of security regulators must develop clear and universal accounting standards with wide-spread international recognition.

Actions at the National and Local Levels

All governments should operate in a transparent and accountable maner at all levels, with the public having access to information to the maximum extent possible. They should ensure that public accounts are open to public scrutiny. The role of civil society is most crucial at the national and local levels, where participation should be fostered by providing open access to decision-makers and the holding of public hearings on matters of importance.

All governments must assure the independence, integrity and depoliticisation of the judicial system as the cornerstone of the rule of law on which the effectiveness of all efforts to combat corruption depends.

The Office of Ombudsman, can make a major contribution to the elimination of bureaucratic obstruction and corruption. Governments, in conjunction with civil society and the private sector, should periodically review the accountability features of all relevant organs of the state and of constitutional office-holders, and at the local level, to ensure that these form an effective bulwark against corruption. Conflict of interest rules must receive special attention.

Governments who have not already done so must restrict to the minimum remaining economic opportunities for bribery and corruption, such as monopolies, discretionary fees, onerous taxes, and regulations and licences that impede business activity.

Countries should improve the effectiveness of their laws dealing with corruption to the maximum extent possible consistent with their constitutions and international human rights norms including:

Abolishing any requirement to prove that an official who received an illegal gift actually gave favours in return.

Providing a system for the declaration of assets by persons holding public positions of trust (and their families).

Introducing the periodic or random monitoring of the assets and life-styles of significant decision-makers in the public sector (and their families and associates), where appropriate by an independent agency:

Laws which effectively empower the freezing, seizure and confiscation of the illicitly acquired wealth of officials found guilty of corruption, wherever it may be and by whomsoever it may be held;

Providing appropriate protection for witness (and their families) and protecting whistle blowers;

Providing system for the recording of gifts received by officials; and

Bearing convicted criminals from standing for political office and appointment to positions of public trust.

Bidders who bribe officials in efforts to win tenders should be blacklisted from competing for official business for an appropriate period, following a fair investigation.

As corruption is a major impediment in the electoral and political processes, urgent action must be taken to implement effective ways in which donations to politicians and political parties are regulated and promptly publicly recorded, and compaign spending limits set and strictly audited. Continuing civic education programmes are essential.

National professional associations, in particular of lawyers, accountants and engineers, must examine the adequacy and effectiveness of their codes of professional conduct and of the means of disciplining those members who facilities corruption.

The role of an independent media is essential, but to function effectively there must be freedom from harassment, freedom of information laws (for citizens and journalists alike) and a legal system which cannot be misused to muzzle legitimate expressions of concern.

Newspaper editors everywhere should reflect on the roles their publications can play in giving the public a "Voice" to counter corruption. Governments, schools and religious institutions should launch education initiatives designed to raise awareness in the young of the incalculable harm done by corruption, and of the personal risks they run of being involved in this.

Codes of conduct should be introduced in many spheres of life (including cabinet, parliament, the judiciary and throughout government ministries), and governments should examine arrangements whereby the ethics and integrity of their administrations can be assured.

We request the Chair of the Conference together with the Secretariat of the International Anti-Corruption Council, Transparency International (TIO) to take the necessary actions to bring these recommendations to the attention of governments and relevant institutions. We pledge that we, ourselves, will do our part.

Adopted from Bulletin of *Lok Sevak Sangh* September, 1997.

23

VALUE EDUCATION AND METHOD OF IMPLEMENTATION IN SCHOOLS

—CITIZEN DEVELOPMENT SOCIETY*

The Purpose of Values in Education

The aim of education is to impart knowledge, to inculcate skills to fit people for work in adult life and above all to help young people develop as full human beings, equipped to lead the good life. In this task Values play a major role as values aim at what Chardin called 'huminization', realising the higher reaches of man's potential that presupposes freedom and imply a vision of good life. However, when we mean values in education, we mean 'Value Oriented Education' and not 'Education of values'. It is the same difference between 'Computer Oriented Education' and 'Education in Computers'. In the first 'Value' is used as adjective whereas in the latter it denotes an area.

Broad Objectives of Value Oriented Education

1. To promote in children such basic and fundamental qualities such as truthfulness, love and compassion, peace and non-violence, courage, equality, justice etc.
2. To train children to become responsible citizens in their personal and social lives.
3. To enable them to become open and considerate in their thought and behaviour and rise above prejudices based on religion, language, caste or sex.
4. To develop proper attitudes towards one's own self and

* 1, West Kidwai Nagar, New Delhi - 110023

fellow beings.

Criteria for Identifying Beliefs, Attitudes, Activities or Feelings as 'Values'

1. It has been freely chosen.
2. It is chosen from one or more available alternatives.
3. It is chosen after due reflection independent of impulse or emoticnal choices.
4. It is prized and cherished.
5. It has been confirmed by others.
6. It has been incorporated into actual behaviour.
7. It is repeated in one's life.

Kinds of Values

Broadly speaking the entire gamut of values may be classified into two types—eternal/absolute or root and temporal/mundane. Moral and spiritual values are root values which take us out of ourselves and inspire us to be good and to do good to others. The mundane values include contextual values-social, cultural, economic etc. The number of values range from three (*Satyam, Shivam, Sundaram*) to 84 (listed by NCERT).

All values are not eternal in nature and are situation, priority, consequence etc. For example 'Honesty is the best Policy' or '*Narova Kunjaro*' from *Mahabharata.*

Educational Values

Desirable educational values are:

1. *Aesthetic*—Arts, dancing, painting, dramatisation, music etc.
2. *Spiritual*—Spirits, opposed to matter, divine matter & soul.
3. *Moral*—Relating to ethics.
4. *Social*—Concerning society and its well being.

Values to be Inculcated at Primary and Secondary School Levels

1. Courage, 2. Truth, 3. Universal love, 4. Respect for all religions,

5. Respect for elders, 6. Dignity of manual work, 7. Service, 8. Purity, 9. Peace, and 10. Joy.

Implementation Strategies

Can values be taught in a formal way? Not entirely. They have to be 'Caught' in environment. They are to be lived. Like a science course, they have to be practised in the home/society laboratory. One 'ounce' of value experience is worth a pound of formal course. Just as swimming cannot be taught merely by lectures, and a good teacher of swimming has to be swimmer himself, similar a teacher of values should himself be a seeker and aspirant of values.

The general strategies followed for inculcation (not teaching) of values are Awareness, Debate, Rational, Concept and Game strategies. It is for teacher to decide which strategy to follow depending upon the situation and the level of students.

School Plan for Teachers for Inculcation of Values

1. All teachers are teachers of value education whether they are formally involved or not in the programme.
2. The school atmosphere, the personality and behaviour of teachers, the facilities provided in the school have a large say in developing a sense of values.
3. The consciousness of values must permeate the whole curriculum (not just value course), formal or non-formal, starting with assembly, the curricular and co-curricular activities, the celebrations of festivals, work experience, team games and sports, subject clubs, social services programmes etc. At present the school atmosphere only conducts such activities as a routine with the purpose of giving information, knowledge and skills without exposing underlying values inherent in them.
4. There should be integrated approach in value education programme. Instead of tackling peace-meal such as awareness of ecology, environmental problem, Community development, productivity etc. they should be handled in a comprehensive manner under the broad spectrum of social responsibility and inner development of human personality.

5. A certain percentage of marks may be assigned at the time of annual examination for some of the values like honesty, social service etc.
6. Introduction of honour system, in the hands of students, with the guidance of teachers.
7. Utilisation of available folklore, national monuments, forms of folk culture to imbibe a sense of belonging.
8. Learner & Faculty interaction to appreciate and understand innovations and initiatives of voluntary efforts. Those working voluntarily for deprived and down trodden could be invited.
9. Inviting persons of unipeachable character, creative abilities, literacy tastes, scholarly activities whose mere presence could innovate children.
10. All functions, programmes, celebrations, gatherings need to ensure that no group or community feels neglected or isolated.
11. To make the school responsive to emergent situations like floods, fire, droughts etc.
12. Visits to institutions, establishments, centres of creative arts, museums etc. and to homes for the aged, blind, handicaped not only enhance knowledge, understanding but-genuine appreciation and empathy.
13. Cleanliness within school helps, in a long way, every individual. Development of aesthetic sensibilities is a basic imperative of individual efforts and group efforts need to be disseminated and discussed. They create lasting impressions.
14. Examples from social life of schools and community that reinforce human aspects of individual efforts and group efforts need to be disseminated and discussed. They create lasting impressions.
15. The teachers should discuss among themselves, during lunch or recess, new incidents in schools which should form 'case histories' for value education programme which will be based on real life situations in the school.
16. To innovate new techniques and methods to understand changes taking place in society. The stress they produce needs to be monitored and the value inculcation programme suitably modified to meet such stresses.

17. 'Ideal School' is a 'Second home' and the teachers are parents in absentia, and should give the same education to other children as they would like to give to their own children.
18. Teachers, Principals and other staff should take formal Oath of allengience to the ethics of their profession like other professions.

REFERENCES

1. *Current-Trends and Problems of Progressive Education*, N.L. Gupta, 1985.
2. *Value Inculcation through Teacher Training*, J.S. Rajpur, University News, March 1993.
3. *Moral Education—A Handbook for Teacher*, R.T. Hall.
4. *Value Oriented School Education*, H.T. Ramji.
5. NCERT Literature.

ADDITIONAL NOTE ON VALUE EDUCATION PROMOTION

—CITIZEN DEVELOPMENT SOCIETY

Value crisis is a global phenomenon of our times. Rapid scientific growth and technological advancements resulting in industrialisation have threatened our ageold moral standards. Disputes over petty matters, dacoities, murders, agitations, stabbing and other crimes are rampant as we read in the newspapers and listen to the media. This atmosphere of valuelessness is leading to disintegration of societies though we notice, at the same time, best of progress in certain other fields. We are also facing today multi-dimensional hazards which were never visualised before. Nietzche rightly remarked, "When a tree grows up to heaven, its roots reach down to hell". We must realise that this process of value deterioration will prove disastrous and lead to disintegration of the society. It is the right time, therefore, for us to rise to action and make conscious efforts to reverse the trend and lead the societies to the right direction.

The first step in the direction of changing the world is to take needed steps for radical change in the human consciousness. One of the most important means to achieve this end is Value Orientation of Education. This will help human beings to conduct themselves in the more desirable directions and to shape their life patterns by strengthening their beliefs and by integrating facts, ideas, attitudes and actions. This will also help them to clarify their aims in life as well as the processes to achieve the same.

It must be recalled that the theme of value education in the traditional sense is synonymous with religious education and moral education. But in the modern context of our commitment to secularism and other such related constitutional provisions, value education is considered much wider so as to transcend the boundaries of religions and encompass, ethical, social, aesthetic, cultural and spiritual values. This broadened concept has many implications for value education programmes at the school stage.

The National Policy of Education has also stated, that. Unfortunately Value Education has received merely lip service so far, though without an effective value education, the country will face crisis of character, adversely affecting the quality of life and relationship leading to tensions and strifes. The economy and development of the country also stand to lose.

The main aim of value education in schools should be to make the students good citizens so that they may share their responsibilities for the development of the country. Students should also be able to understand the national goals of democracy, secularism and socialism. They could develop themselves to be useful fellow citizens and continuously strive for their inner development.

The Citizenship Development Society is bringing out publication to help the schools in implementing the strategies for imparting values to the students. CDS has been sincerely devoted to the task of value orientation of education. It has organised more than 35 seminars/orientation courses and Regional Seminars-cum-Workshops on value education. Thus the Society has committed itself to spread the message and to promote value education in the school system.

24

HUMAN VALUES AND THE ROTARY SYSTEM

—RTN MANJIT S. SAWHNEY*

From a letter to all Team Mates dated October 18, 1997 on the subject of JAGRITI—INTERCITY ON VALUES, I have written and I quote:

"Fifty year of our Independence is perhaps not a long time in the history of a nation to judge its progress. But fifty years is ample time to understand the psyche of a people—the attitude of a nation. Over three months as I have toured our District I have become very conscious of the extreme agitation and frustration in the minds of Rotarians regarding the erosion of values that is visible in every sphere of our national life. Therefore, I have decided to dedicate the second Intercity—*Jagriti*—The Awakening, to this vital issue. Rotary Club of Delhi Southend hopes to make this an Intercity with a difference—an Intercity we in District 3010 would remember for a long time.

Thus Human Values concerns us all. It is a Task for All. Hence in the following Paragraphs is quoted my message to all fellow Rotarians;

A great river is the sum total of contributions of hundreds, perhaps thousand of little brooks and rivulets which come tumbling down the hill sides and mountains singing as they go, eager to cast themselves into the channel of the great river. That is like the Growth of Rotary. It has become great because of the self sacrificing contributions of thousands of Rotarians of many lands. As

* District Governor 1997-98, Rotary International Dist. 3010.

we prepare to serve Rotary in 1997-98, we need a guiding beacon—A common focus on which we can chart our course of building a better world through better communities. Our programme for next year is ambitious and challenging but it can be simply expressed in the words of our theme for the year:

"SHOW ROTARY CARES"

This is what RI President Glen Kinross has asked every Rotarian in every community to do during the year ahead.

Show Rotary Cares	—	By working to feed the hungry.
Show Rotary Cares	—	By helping to lift people out of poverty.
Show Rotary Cares	—	By providing every adult with basic reading and mathematical skills.
Show Rotary Cares	—	By protecting innocent children from abuse and neglect.
Show Rotary Cares	—	By undertaking projects for your community that will make your cities and towns a better place in which to live and work..
Show Rotary Cares	—	For vocational service by encouraging every Rotarian to uphold the Highest ethical standards in business and professions always putting principle above expediency.

I ask each Rotarian of Dist. 3010 to walk the paths of Rotary with me in 1997-98 with courage concern and commitment.

The four way Test of things, we think, say or do:

(1) Is it the *Truth*?
(2) Is it *Fair* to all concerned?
(3) Will it build *Goodwill* and *Better Friendship*?
(4) Will it be *Beneficial* to all concerned?

The Objects of the Rotary

The object of Rotary is to encourage and foster the ideal of service as a basis of worthy enterprise and, in particular, to encourage and foster:

First: The development of acquaintance as an opportunity for service;

Second: High Ethical Standards in business and professions; the recognition of worthiness of all useful occupations; and dignifying by each Rotarian of his occupation as an opportunity to serve society;

Third: The application of the ideal of service by every Rotarian to his personal, business and community life;

Fourth: The advancement of international understanding, goodwill and peace through a world fellowship of business and professional persons united in the ideal of service.

I would like each and every Rotarian to be involved since this subject of Human Values concerns us all, it is a task for us all.

Rtn. Manjit S. Sawhney